God's Grace:
Not an Easy Promise

Rose Block

Bloomington, IN Milton Keynes, UK

AuthorHouse™
1663 Liberty Drive, Suite 200
Bloomington, IN 47403
www.authorhouse.com
Phone: 1-800-839-8640

AuthorHouse™ UK Ltd.
500 Avebury Boulevard
Central Milton Keynes, MK9 2BE
www.authorhouse.co.uk
Phone: 08001974150

This book is a work of non-fiction. Unless otherwise noted, the author and the publisher make no explicit guarantees as to the accuracy of the information contained in this book and in some cases, names of people and places have been altered to protect their privacy.

© 2006 Rose Block. All rights reserved.

No part of this book may be reproduced, stored in a retrieval system, or transmitted by any means without the written permission of the author.

First published by AuthorHouse   12/5/2006

ISBN: 978-1-4259-8093-1 (sc)

Library of Congress Control Number: 2006910347

Unless otherwise noted all Scripture Quotations are from The New International Version of the Bible.

Printed in the United States of America
Bloomington, Indiana

This book is printed on acid-free paper.

Dedication

This book is dedicated first and foremost to my heavenly Father, my God and Savior who reigns above all in my life. I pray His anointing on this book and those who read it. I feel He has called me to share this story of His faithfulness and love, and has delivered the words through me. May all honor and glory be given to Him.

Secondly, I dedicate this book to my loving husband, Joe. He has walked faithfully by my side throughout the past nineteen years. My life was blessed the day God brought him into it. Joe is my best friend and soul mate. He has been my greatest encourager on this project.

And lastly, I dedicate this book to my mother, Helen Vogelsong. My mother is a true woman of faith. She has supported me, loved me, and taught me many lessons by her example. The grace of God has been ever present in her life. To know my mother is to know the Lord. The love, joy, and peace in her life are a result of walking close with her almighty God.

Introduction

I walked down the halls of Hershey Medical Center, and everything—from the rushed nurses and doctors to the antiseptic smell—seemed all too familiar. I'd been here many times before; some of the happiest, and saddest, days of my life had been spent inside these walls. Four of our children were born in this hospital. Each birth became an amazing journey of new life and excitement.

For years, this hospital held only the fondest memories until I started bringing my sister here for doctor appointments and cancer treatments. She was only forty-two when the Lord took her home to be with Him in January of 2000.

God used her painful journey to touch and mature many people, especially me, in faith and dependence on Him. While I helped my sister through her difficult ordeal, God began teaching me about His strength and grace. How could I know that He was preparing me for a storm that lay directly ahead—a storm no parent could ever imagine, let alone survive without His mercy and grace.

In October 2005, I visited the hospital once more for a sad event—to say good-bye to a dear friend, 83-year-old Dottie Heagy, whom I'd met in the hospital more than five years before. She had had a heart attack, and I knew it would be just a matter of time before God took her home.

During the visit, the nurse asked me to step out of the room. I complied with her request and was drawn to the elevator just a few steps away. A sudden need to go to the seventh floor overwhelmed me. I moved toward the elevator doors knowing full well the memories I was about to unleash. I stepped inside and pressed the button. The elevator moved upward. When the doors opened, I returned to some of the most painful days of my life—the Penn State Children's Hospital, which is also the seventh floor of Hershey Medical Center.

Our four-year-old daughter, Ashley, had spent twelve days in the Pediatric Intensive Care Unit on this floor in May 2000.

I stepped out of the elevator and walked down the hall. Memories came flooding back. I observed the waiting room with its wall-to-wall chairs and magazines strewn hastily on tables. This was the room where my family congregated and waited to hear from the doctor about Ashley's condition.

To my right, I saw the two pay phones in the corner, and I relived the anxious calls we made to family and friends every day. My stomach lurched seeing the small coffee table. It brought back memories of the night Joe and I sat in front of it, holding hands, waiting to hear news of our little girl.

At 11:30 p.m., our pastor had walked through the door. He'd received skewed information that Ashley had died.

Grieving for us, he had come to comfort Joe and me, but upon learning she was still alive, he counseled us on how a tragedy can affect a marriage.

On my way back to the elevator, I passed several families knitted together in love. It was obvious they were awaiting news about their loved ones. Just five years ago, our family sat in those very same chairs.

Over the years, I had repressed the memory of Ashley's accident. It seemed like a whole lifetime ago. But now, back in the hospital, the memories seemed vivid and real. The sight of nurses scurrying along hallways rushing toward their charges made it seem like just yesterday that I had stood here in the middle of my storm.

At the elevator, I stood patiently and waited for it to arrive. I glanced out the window to my left and remembered one more thing. Shortly after Ashley's accident, I stood in that very spot. It had rained earlier—outside, and in my heart—but when I looked out the window, I saw a beautiful rainbow, curved across a pale, blue sky.

I will never leave you nor forsake you. God's words were as clear as that rainbow. He spoke to me, and I knew how faithful He'd always been. I had no doubt He would walk with me through this tragedy. I can't begin to relate the comfort He provided.

With a sigh, I left the memories behind and pushed the elevator button. I returned to the sixth floor where I went to see our adopted Grandma Dottie for the very last time.

My story is a testimony of God's grace as he carried our family through one of the toughest storms a parent can experience—a life-threatening accident involving a child.

The first section of *God's Grace: Not an Easy Promise* is a recap of the events of the evening in May when Ashley suffered a near-fatal bicycle accident (Part 1: The Event), followed by my journal entries during our hospital stay (Part 2: Finding Peace within Chaos). The last portion will relate the lessons God taught us through our awful storm (Part 3: Lessons Learned).

Looking back, I'm thankful the worst day of our lives became a new beginning, not only for me but for our entire family. My prayer is that your eyes might be opened to the abundance and goodness of God's grace in your life through both good times and bad. He is waiting for us to come to Him, trust in Him, and allow His strength to be our strength. The Lord says, "My grace is sufficient for you . . ." (2 Cor. 12:9).

Contents

Part 1
The Event that Changed Our Lives Forever

May 8, 2000 3
Hershey Medical Center 9
Pediatric Intensive Care Unit 14

Section 2
Finding Peace within Chaos

Finding Peace within Chaos 23

Journal Entries

    Week One 26
    Week two 29
    Week three 38
    Week four 52
    Week five 59
    Week six 72
    Week seven 78
    Week eight 86
    Going Home! 90
    Months four-nine 103

Part 3
Lessons Learned

Lesson 1: The Power of Prayer 115
Lesson 2: Unshakable Faith 125
Lesson 3: An Attitude of Gratitude 132
Lesson 4: Pursuing Patience 140
Lesson 5: Compassion and Love 143
Lesson 6: Loving Life 148

PART 1

The Event that Changed Our Lives Forever

May 8, 2000

May 8, 2000, began as a fantastic day.

Joe and I, married almost thirteen years, had three beautiful children. Andrew, six, was almost through his first year of kindergarten. At four years old, Ashley was starting to blossom into a beautiful little girl, and Michael, just shy of two, had a warm sense of humor that brightened our home with love and laughter.

Over the past six years, the elevator business Joe and his dad owned had finally become fruitful, and we decided to bring another child into our family. Years before, I had resigned from teaching and enjoyed staying home with our children.

The decision about another child made my life complete. Life couldn't have been any better. Each night before I went to bed, I quietly walked into each child's room and kissed them. I pulled the covers around them and prayed to God, thanking Him for our many blessings. Some nights, I felt overwhelmed by His goodness, and I would offer my family and myself back to Him to be used for His glory. God knew my heart was genuine, and I would give anything I had to Him—even my family.

On May 8, one of the first really warm nights of spring, Joe came home from work, and we had a quick dinner together before he rushed off to the golf course with some buddies.

He kissed each of us good-bye once, then again when the kids asked for another round of kisses. We were still sitting at the dinner table when he headed out the door.

I usually cleaned up from dinner and started an early bedtime routine of baths, story, and lights out since it was a school night for Andrew. But because the evening was so beautiful with the sun dropping lazily behind the horizon, I asked the kids if they wanted to take a quick bicycle ride to the stop sign and back before getting their baths. In a chorus, they all said "yes."

"Could we please go around the development together?" Andrew asked. Ashley soon joined his pleading. She adored her older brother and united forces in anything he requested. I agreed. Before long, the kids had their helmets on and were climbing on their bicycles.

Andrew was confident riding his bike since he often rode with his daddy, and Ashley had a new Barbie bicycle with training wheels that she'd received a few short months before for her fourth birthday. My youngest, Michael, sat in a child seat on the back of my bicycle.

We took off on our ride, passing many neighbors who were also outside enjoying the pleasant evening. The breeze tousled my hair, and my thoughts turned to the magnificent evening.

What a beautiful night! Life just can't get any better than this.

We started down a hill, one we had ridden down many times before. But this time, instead of walking beside Ashley to steady her, I was on my own bike. When Ashley's bike began picking up speed, I felt a lump grow in my throat.

Oh, Lord, please stop her!

I couldn't help my little girl and watched in disbelief as she tried to position her small feet on the tumbling pedals, but couldn't. The pedals propelled faster and faster, and she couldn't stop them.

"Pull onto the grass, Ashley!" I shouted. "Pull onto the grass!" My mind reeled as quickly as Ashley's tires spun out of control, taking her to an unknown destination. I felt helpless. There was nothing I could do.

Suddenly, a vehicle came from nowhere and idled at the bottom of the hill. The driver saw her coming and had to make a split-second decision—should he move out of her way or remain stopped at the stop sign hoping she would turn and miss him? Quickly, he hit the gas, trying to clear her path. He didn't, and with full force, Ashley collided with the back of his truck. The collision threw her onto the road where she lay crumpled and lifeless.

It happened so quickly. One minute, life was gorgeous and full of promise, and the next, I was faced with the thought of saying good-bye to my precious little girl. I threw my bike onto the grass and sprinted down the hill. I took one look at Ashley, and I had three thoughts: Call 911, call Joe, and call God!

Neighbors started to gather and gawked at the scene before them. I raced to the nearest house and banged on the door. "Please, can I use your phone? My daughter's hurt!" I felt my face flush, and I fought back tears.

I must keep calm. Ashley's life depends on it.

I dialed 911 as quickly as possible. The operator listened to my plea and said, "An ambulance is on the way."

After I hung up the phone, I looked out the glass door and saw a neighbor who loved the Lord as much as we did. I ran to him.

"W-Will you please pray with me, Kurt?"

I heard Kurt's voice in the background, pleading with God to protect Ashley from harm. At the same time, I was frantically trying to recall Joe's cell number. After Kurt's heartfelt prayer, I called Joe. He must have been busy on the golf course because it took awhile before he answered.

My heart was racing, and I stuttered, "J-Joe, it's Ashley. She's run into a truck. She was riding her bicycle . . ."

When he asked if she was all right, I simply said, "No."

Later, I wondered what went through Joe's mind. He was in the middle of a golf course, miles away from home when I called and gave him the bad news that his daughter had collided with a truck.

I raced back to Ashley. Hours seemed to pass while I waited for the ambulance. I paced back and forth along the side of the road. Ashley lay on the asphalt road unconscious and barely breathing.

"Ashley, breathe!" I commanded, and she gulped down some air. Her chest rose and fell a few quick times, then went still again.

Not only did God send Kurt at the right moment, He sent another angel to the scene—Bob. Bob knelt beside Ashley's almost lifeless body and whispered, "Stay with us, Ashley. Stay with us, sweetie." His unusual ability to remain calm under the circumstances kept me calm. Without Bob,

I might have grabbed Ashley, and held her close, possibly causing further injury.

In hindsight, I wonder if we should have used CPR on her while we waited for the paramedics. To their credit, doctors and nurses have assured me that if no one at the scene knew how to correctly do the special CPR for severe head injuries, we could have made her condition worse.

Lord, am I keeping it together? Or is Your amazing hand of grace keeping me from losing it?

Within minutes the ambulance, its siren wailing, careened down the street.

Several paramedics rushed to Ashley's side, quickly started IVs, and prepared her to travel.

One EMT asked, "Which hospital?" In minutes, they decided on Lancaster General. I don't know how I knew, but something in my spirit said she needed to go to Hershey Medical Center if she had any hope of survival. When I told them, they agreed without any debate.

I followed close behind the stretcher as the paramedics loaded Ashley into the ambulance. Right before I joined them, one of the men said, "I'm sorry, you can't ride in the ambulance."

"B-but, I'm her mother. She needs me."

"I'm sorry, we already have too many in the back trying to keep her alive. You need to follow us." With that, he closed the door.

It felt as though he'd closed the door on my little girl's life.

Lord, I can't be strong anymore. I can't hold it together . . .
I began screaming. Tears streaked my face as I tried to open the doors. "I've got to go with Ashley! She'll breathe if I tell her. I've got to go!"

The next thing I knew, two strong arms pulled me from the back of the ambulance.

In the confusion, I looked up to see another ambulance. I raced toward it, so I could ride with them, but those paramedics were already in the back of Ashley's ambulance.

What is the real reason I can't go? Do they think Ashley may die before she gets to the hospital?

Everything happened so quickly. Sobbing hysterically, it took several people to calm me down.

I was still crying when Joe pulled into the development. He saw the ambulance driving away, and a river of blood flowing across the street where Ashley's little body had lain. We later learned that Ashley had bled quite a bit from her ears, which turned out to be a good thing since it limited the swelling and damage.

"Is she dead?" Joe asked. His face was ashen, and he was visibly shaken. When no one answered, he raced toward me.

"What's going on, Rose?" He still wore his khaki shorts from playing golf. When he learned that Ashley was still alive, he grabbed my hand.

Hershey Medical Center

Neither of us was in any condition to drive, and a neighbor offered to drive us to the hospital. Hershey Medical Center was only fifteen minutes away, but it felt like forever. The ambulance sped off in a hurry and soon disappeared. So, we made our way through traffic like anyone else. The ride was extremely quiet. Neither Joe nor I knew what to say.

Then he asked the question I dreaded. "How did this happen, Rose?"

Thankfully, he didn't place any guilt or blame on me; he just needed to know the details. I answered his question to the best of my ability, and the ride went quiet again. I prayed a lot on the way to Hershey.

Oh Father, please save Ashley! I begged.

I punched numbers into my cell phone, but all I got was message machine after message machine. No one was available. It seemed as if everyone else was outside enjoying the beautiful warm spring evening.

I did, however, get through to two people. One was a friend from church, Kim. She belonged to our mom's playgroup and was a mighty prayer warrior.

"Oh, Kim," I said, sobbing. "I'm so glad I got you. Please call the pastor and tell him that Ashley had a serious accident. Then call everyone else. Ask them to pray that she lives." Kim calmed me down, so I could call the next person on my list—my mom.

I dreaded talking to my mother because I didn't want to upset her. I desperately wanted her at the hospital with me, but I was afraid to tell her what happened, and just how serious it was.

Only four short months before, we had to bury her daughter, my sister, when she lost her battle with cancer. How hard to ask Mom to go back to the same hospital that held so many painful memories. The heartache was still fresh—for all of us.

When my mother's cheerful voice came on the phone, I took a deep breath.

"Mom," I said, "Ashley was in a bicycle accident, and we're taking her to Hershey. Can you meet us there?" Without hesitation, she answered yes.

I was thankful she didn't ask me for any details about the accident or Ashley's condition. I'm sure, however, that I didn't fool my mother. She probably knew it was serious. After hanging up, I continued to pray.

As soon as we arrived at the hospital, a doctor and a heavyset chaplain met us. My heart felt as if it had crawled up in my throat. *She's gone. My baby is gone. Why else would a chaplain come to meet us?*

The doctor spoke first. "Ashley's still alive."

"I don't believe you," I said, and then I looked squarely at the chaplain. "Then why is *he* here if she's still alive?"

The chaplain cleared his throat. "I'm called in on all traumas," he said, "especially when a child is involved."

I felt somewhat better. Joe and I followed them to a small room, separate from the regular waiting room, where we could wait together as a family until the doctor could talk with us.

It wasn't long before people began arriving to show their support and be available if we needed anything. I couldn't remain still, and I paced back and forth in the small hallway adjacent to the waiting room.

Joe and I didn't talk much. Each of us was trying to process the last hour's events and trying desperately not to think about possible outcomes.

As I continued to pace the hall, I felt overjoyed seeing my mother walking to meet me. I remember her hugging me and together we said a verse we'd memorized and repeated time after time during my sister Barb's terrible illness: "Do not be anxious about anything, but in everything, by prayer and petition, with thanksgiving, present your requests to God. And the peace of God, which transcends all understanding, will guard your hearts and your minds in Christ Jesus" (Phil. 4:6,7). She hugged me again. Then we prayed together and asked God to please save Ashley's life.

Later that night in the waiting room, Joe and I prayed. *Please dear God, save our little girl. We will take her any way You decide, but please don't let her die.*

While we pleaded with God to save Ashley, we also were very aware that He was in control of the situation.

Later that night, I sat in one of the waiting room chairs quietly singing the praise song, "God is So Good to Me." Then, I sang the second verse. When I finished singing that verse quietly to myself, I heard my friend Kim begin another verse of the song, the one that says how God answers prayer. Until that time, I hadn't even realized anyone was sitting beside me, but that verse alone gave me much peace and comfort, plus a little bit of hope.

As the night wore on, people continued to show up at the hospital to sit with us. Thankfully, most of my family arrived. It meant so much to be surrounded by family and friends, neighbors and pastors. My one sister, Sharon, didn't come to the hospital, but she played more of a role in my peace that night than she will ever realize.

Sharon was very close to my boys and had spent a lot of time with them. She volunteered to go to my house and be with them while we were in the hospital. They knew her well, and I knew they would be comforted by her presence. I needed to know someone I trusted stayed with my other children and could handle any questions or situations. It freed my mind to concentrate solely on Ashley.

After several hours, the doctors came to talk to us, and what they said wasn't good.

The taller doctor spoke first, very slowly and deliberately, "Ashley has broken all the bones in the base of her skull, and tissue has torn away from the brain stem." He explained that a brain stem injury is the most serious type of head injury and when the tissue tears from it, the outcome is not favorable.

"I'd like to wait until tomorrow morning to talk about all the details," he said, "and that's only if Ashley survives the night." When no one spoke up, he went on, "If she does survive, we would be talking about a severe brain injury, possibly complete paralysis, and she may never come off the ventilator."

Everyone in the room was stunned. Absolutely and totally stunned. I don't recall anything we said to the doctor, or our family and friends. After the doctor left the room, our pastor was very wise and considerate.

"Could everyone please step out of the room?" he asked. I was relieved when the last person left the room so Joe and I could be alone.

I looked into my husband's weary eyes. Tears bubbled up and began to slide down his face. It was the first time he'd cried. I knew he felt like I did, and that we might lose our precious little girl; it was more than we could comprehend. Together we sat alone and wept.

After a long while, Joe spoke first. "Ashley belongs to God, you know," he said, trying to stem the tears that flowed, and wiping them with the back of his hand. "And if He decides to take her home then we need to be thankful for the four wonderful years He gave us."

I didn't want to admit Joe was right, and I didn't want Ashley to die, but the sooner I saw the truth as Joe spoke it, the easier it was for me to trust God and take each minute as it came. United in God's strength, the two of us pulled ourselves together and walked out of the room, unified as a team.

Pediatric Intensive Care Unit

The night wore on, and I lost track of the minutes and hours. It was some time before Joe and I saw the gurney roll past that held our little girl. The doctors had stabilized Ashley enough to move her upstairs to the Pediatric Intensive Care Unit (PICU).

For a few moments, I looked down at her and prayed, "Please, Lord, take care of Ashley. Let her live. We will take her back any way You choose, just don't let her die."

As the nurse pushed the gurney past us, I saw an arm or leg (I don't remember which) move. At the time, I didn't realize how important that simple movement was, but the doctor did. Her ability to move any of her limbs was a good sign she didn't have a spinal cord injury. That meant they could rule out the possibility of complete paralysis. *Praise God!* The next twenty-four to seventy-two hours would be critical. At any time, her brain could swell so much it couldn't be contained. If that occurred, nothing else could be done, and she would die.

The nurse wheeled Ashley to the elevator; and in a blink, she was out of sight again. I didn't know if I'd ever see my little girl again. The only thing I could do was trust in God and continue to pray.

The nurse took Ashley to the seventh floor, the Pediatric Intensive Care Unit, and it would be another couple of hours before we could see her.

On the seventh floor, we sat in a large waiting room where we could all be more comfortable. I don't remember how many people had gathered to support Joe and me, but I knew it was a lot, and I found it comforting.

I knew that as soon as Ashley woke up, she would ask for her bun-bun and her blanket, and I asked Joe's nephew, Tommy, if he would please run home and get them. I needed to know I had her blanket and bunny ready as soon as she wanted them.

Eventually, a nurse came to get Joe and me. Her voice was gentle as she said, "You can go back to see her now."

The doctors and nurses tried to prepare us for what we would see. They said it would be difficult. Upon entering Ashley's room, however, I didn't think she looked bad. She just looked like my beautiful little girl. She didn't have any cuts or scrapes on her body from the accident, and she lay on the bed quite peaceful, sound asleep. But when I looked at all the machines and equipment used to keep her alive, I had a sick feeling in the pit of my stomach. I knew instantly we needed to pray.

I left the room to gather my family to pray over her. It was reminiscent of our time with Barb when we held hands and prayed—united in Jesus' name. I wanted and needed to pray like that again—for our little sweetheart. My family and Pastor Heath followed me to Ashley's room. About ten or eleven of us stood around her bed.

Pastor Heath laid his hand on her head, closed his eyes, and began to pray fervently for her survival and recovery. When he finished and removed his hand, I began to see God work in a big, big way. Although we didn't understand at first what was happening, we realized later that God revealed his power.

Ashley's ICP (inter-cranial pressure) had stabilized and was at a safe number of 20, which was why they allowed us to visit her. As soon as the pastor removed his hand from her head, Ashley's numbers shot up to 66. The alarms sounded, and the nurses rushed everyone out of the room. They put medicine in her IV and prepared her for an emergency CAT scan.

We were told there were three different things they could try to reduce the pressure in her brain. They had just used the first of three options. It concerned them greatly that her numbers had spiked so quickly. There were only two things left to control the swelling; after that, there would be nothing more they could do. We were told we could lose her at any point in the next seventy-two hours. What mostly concerned the doctors was they had already used one of the medicines at this early stage. The majority of swelling does not even begin until twenty-four hours following an injury. The emergency CAT scan would reveal if something new were going on inside her brain.

We were asked to step back into the hallway while they prepared her for travel the second time. Once again, we watched them wheel our little girl past us. This time, someone rode on the gurney with Ashley and continued to "bag her" in order to keep her lungs filled with air. As a mother, it was difficult to see Ashley hooked up to so much equipment.

Later, we were told the CAT scan showed some very important information. Fluid had begun to gather in the four ventricles of her brain, fluid that was *not* there previously when they had done the original scan. They told us they needed to insert a shunt into her brain so they could drain any additional fluid buildup. The shunt insertion went as expected, and the doctors now had a way to keep the fluid buildup to a minimum. Ashley's ICP numbers returned to a safe 20, and she stabilized once again.

After this latest episode, I stood and held my little girl's hand. I felt the presence of God, and I felt Him say, *Do you know who was behind Ashley's numbers spiking and the emergency CAT scan?*

Before I could answer, it was if He said, *I am in control, and I know what my child needs.* Suddenly, everything became clear. God had caused Ashley's numbers to go haywire to get the doctor's attention. Had they not done the emergency scan that night, fluid would have gathered and caused additional irreversible brain damage. God is a big God and has a way of making His voice heard.

So many times we think we need to take control of our situations and become God's voice even when we don't have a clue what decisions we are trifling with. When we put God in a box, we fail to see His ability to act and speak. We limit the many blessings He so desires to give us. God spoke in such a way that the doctors listened.

The next seventy-two hours would be extremely critical. Ashley was in bad shape and only time would reveal the outcome of this terrible tragedy. Word spread quickly about Ashley's accident, and everyone who heard of it wanted to help in any way possible. At this point there wasn't a whole lot any of us could do but pray, and that's what we did.

At the beginning of the twenty-four to seventy-two hour period, people gathered at our church in Elizabethtown, Pennsylvania, to pray. About seventy-five people showed up that evening. The prayer vigil lasted about an hour. The pastor divided the large group into several smaller groups and gave each one a different area in which to pray; some prayed for Ashley, some prayed for Joe and me, some prayed for our family, some prayed for the neighbor who was driving the truck, and some prayed for the doctors' wisdom and skills. The amount of people praying for Ashley at the vigil (and those not able to make it to the church) was truly amazing. Joe and I are from large families. We have many, many friends and a large church family. Anyone who knew our family and heard of the accident began praying to God for his grace and mercy for Ashley. The prayers definitely made a difference. Ashley's ICP numbers stabilized around 20 (which are very good) and did not rise much during the entire twenty-four to seventy-two hour window. Ashley's head nurse was amazed. She told us she was dreading coming back to work the following day because she knew what could happen during the swelling period.

She was pleasantly surprised to have calm nights with Ashley during the critical period. I remember watching the clock and being focused on the end of the seventy-two hours.

When the period ended, I was talking on the phone with my brother-in-law. I rejoiced with him and finally said good-bye, so I could go into the room to see Ashley. When I walked in, I walked into chaos as Ashley's numbers were rising steadily. Thankfully, they never reached a danger point before they once more began to decline. Again, God spoke to my soul and said, *Now that I have your attention, just remember who got her through that danger zone. I did it; now be sure to give me the glory.* It's amazing when God speaks to you, and you know it. I thanked God for walking beside us each step of the way. I knew Ashley was still in bad shape but felt hope for the first time that we wouldn't have to bury our beautiful little girl.

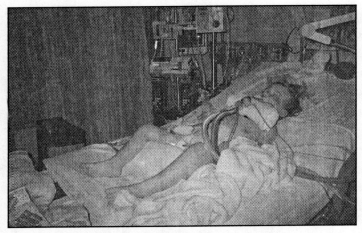

Ashley fought hard just to stay alive
those first 72 hours following her accident.

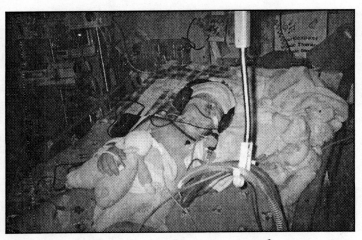

Music therapy was used early on as a way of reconnecting
Ashley to familiar voices and sounds.

Section 2

Finding Peace within Chaos

Finding Peace within Chaos

A few days following the accident, I felt as if I were slipping away. Life had become frenzied, and I didn't know how to stop the confusion in my mind. My family came to the hospital frequently, and I was thankful because they added some stability.

Doctors and nurses filled the hallways in a rush to see their patients, and of course, a member of the hospital staff always seemed to be in Ashley's room.

Much heartache was palpable on the seventh floor. We were not the only family on that floor with a sick or injured child. The longer I remained on the seventh floor, the more I realized the cycle never ended. Other families were constantly coming in with their own tragedies. I found myself not only concerned with my own tragedy, but others' tragedies as well. Sleep became elusive.

One day, my mother insisted I lie down for a while and try to rest. Occasionally that helped, but sometimes it made the craziness surrounding me worse. In the quiet times, my mind still raced, and usually in directions that weren't healthy. But this particular day, I listened to my mother. I was determined to focus only on God's goodness and grace. I knew I needed Him to get through my daughter's accident.

Words formed in my mind—*Finding Peace within Chaos*—the title of a book chapter I planned to write with a friend following Barb's death. We wanted to write the book revealing my faith in God. After Barb died, I knew God called me to write. The only thing my friend and I had accomplished was outlining the chapters—then Ashley had her accident.

It was as if God brought those words back to me in the hospital, "OK, here is the research for the book you are writing. How are you going to find peace?" *How can I find peace? I am in the middle of chaos.* My answer came from Isaiah 26:3, "You will keep in perfect peace him whose mind is steadfast, because he trusts in You."

Lord, I want to commit myself to You, to lean on You, and know You are able to handle this situation.

I wanted that perfect peace in the middle of the chaos. By cooperating with the Holy Spirit and allowing God to pour His grace upon me, I found I could get through each day. Without God, I was a basket case, but with Him I was able to make it. I could even be excited learning what God had to show me.

Not long after Ashley's accident, I became compelled to journal. As you read through the following entries, I pray your eyes will see God's grace and what the Holy Spirit taught me; how He strengthened me and enabled me to persevere during those difficult days.

I must add that we persevered, not because we are naturally strong people; Joe and I are still babies in our faith. We made it because God was working on both of us as He poured out His grace and love when we didn't deserve it. It was by His power that we were able to survive those days and grow despite our circumstances. He alone gets the glory for each and every journal entry you are about to read.

Journal Entries

Week One

Friday, May 12, 2000
8:00 p.m.

>*Four days have passed since Ashley's accident. My emotions run deep as I sit and look at my beautiful daughter lying in a hospital bed. She is fighting for her life with everything that's in her. God blessed her with a strong will, and now I understand why. The doctors say it is a matter of time, and that the healing is up to Ashley. I know in my heart, however, that her healing is in God's hands.*

Saturday, May 13, 2000
4:00 p.m.

>*Ashley had a good night. We started playing some classical music, which seems to soothe and comfort her. On average, her inter-cranial pressure seems to be doing*

better. For the most part, her numbers have stayed in the low teens. However, when the pressure rises, and the ICP numbers go up on the monitor, I feel anxiety rise in my own heart. I just want the numbers to come down and stabilize.

God chose this path for our lives and as much as I wish things were back to normal, we are ready for God to work through us. I read an article today about the limitations that we place on our lives and how we need to give things over to the Lord so He can use our weakness for His glory.

7:00 p.m.

Ashley opened her eyes a little bit. She raised one hand and tried to breathe on her own. With all that effort, her ICP numbers did not go up. Praise God! She also had her first bowel movement, which was another good sign. I am so grateful to God for all He has done. We have repeated one question over and over again— How do people get through ordeals like this without God? He is my Rock.

P.S. I saw a rainbow tonight—the ultimate sign of God's promise!

Sunday, May 14, 2000 – Mother's Day
6:30 a.m.

As the sun rises over the horizon, I stand quietly looking down at my daughter. The only way I can start this day is to thank You, God, for saving our beautiful little girl so I may sit with her and hold her hand on this Mother's Day.

I slept great last night but the second I opened my eyes, my first thought was of Ashley. I practically sprinted down the hall. I only controlled myself because of the other patients. I found Ashley sleeping peacefully this morning with her music playing. Her ICP numbers ranged around 11 or 12.

Joe went to breakfast with Dan this morning. I'm finding the key to staying focused on God is surrounding myself with people who love and fear God. They uplift me when times are tough. Another component to staying focused on God is to be in His Word. It's impossible for God to speak to me through His Word if I'm not in it. The verses in His Word, the Bible, are life-giving and life-changing.

12:00 a.m.

The day is done, and I am exhausted. What started out as a peaceful Mother's Day has ended with lots of uncertainty. I need to write a few words tonight to help me focus on God and reflect on the day. It was a rough one. Emotions ran high most of the time. Ashley's ICP numbers kept jumping around. Ashley had another CT scan which came back pretty good. The doctors think the reason her numbers are staying a little higher is because she is more awake during the day.

I felt very weak at times today. High emotions and physical fatigue are not good partners. I found myself claiming 2 Corinthians 12:10 that says, "... For when I am weak, then I am strong." His grace is sufficient. I could never imagine myself going through something like this with one of my children, and yet I am six days into it. God has certainly been faithful. He is right beside me and is holding Ashley's little body in His arms. It is in Him that I find my strength. I'm very grateful for my friends and family who help me keep focused on God. After all, He is the Great Physician!

Week two

Monday, May 15, 2000
5:45 p.m.

I am cherishing 2 Cor. 12:10 again. "... For when I am weak, then I am strong." I've felt very weak at times today, but I know that it is those times I need to reach for the Lord. Ashley is listening to classical music all the time. Maybe someday she will become one of the world's greatest ballerinas. She always loved her ballet class and now the music will certainly be ingrained in her little mind. She really seems to respond well to the music.

My Uncle John's prayer was very comforting tonight. He prayed for Ashley's healing and strength for Joe and me, and the rest of the family. He also prayed with great thanksgiving for God's faithfulness. All the steps Ashley has made have been in the right direction. God is certainly working and touching the hearts of many people. I thank Him for using my little girl as a tool for His work.

9:00 p.m.

    Ashley seems peaceful right now. It's very quiet and orderly in her room. I enjoy sitting with her at times like this. I know I can help her get better and regain some of the motilities that were lost once she opens her eyes, breathes on her own again, and knows Mommy is with her.

    Mary Beth is coming to sit with me tonight—what a great friend I have in her.

Tuesday, May 16, 2000
8:30 p.m.

    I spent time today reading Barb's journal pages. She left us with such wisdom within those two pages. Some of her words jumped off the page at me this morning:

- God hears each and every prayer.
- I must remember to hand this illness over to God.
- I can never repay the kindness and compassion shown to me but maybe I can touch someone else's life the way so many have reached out to me.
- May I never forget the gift of life and live each day to the fullest.
- May I give thanks for all the little things in life.
- God strengthens us in times of trials and tribulations.
- God, family, and friends are what matter most in this world of turmoil.

God has been teaching me a new lesson. As important as it is to surround myself with family and friends, it's equally important to find some quiet time alone with God. It is during that quiet time that God really has a chance to speak. I have dedicated Ashley to Him. I feel the accident is the path He chose to allow for my family and our lives. I pray He uses us for His work and His glory.

12:00 p.m.

So far, today was one of the hardest days. Ashley went down for a scan and everything seemed to fall apart. Fear and anxiety ran high. I need to remember Philippians 4:6 that tells me not to worry about anything. Sometimes it's hard for our human brains to do that.

Joe and I celebrated our anniversary tonight. Mary Beth and Sonya made dinner for us. We had a very romantic dinner, complete with candlelight, music, and nonalcoholic wine—in the PICU conference room. This will be one anniversary we'll always remember.

Reflecting on the anniversary, I'd have to say it was probably the best one we've ever had. I know people might say, "How in the world can you say that?" But when I really think about it, we still have our beautiful little girl, and Joe and I are closer than we've ever been. God is truly working in both our lives. He is drawing us nearer to Him each day and by doing so, He is strengthening the bond in our marriage.

On the way home from the hospital, Mary Beth and I had a great conversation. (Joe and I take turns going home each night for an hour or so to tuck the boys in bed and keep things somewhat normal for them.) Mary Beth and I talked about the many lessons we have learned so far and the many more God will surely reveal to us and through us to others.

Wednesday, May 17, 2000
10:45 a.m.

Ashley just finished her first C-Pap test, which allows her to breathe on her own for an hour. With the exception of one little episode, she passed the test with flying colors. And to that I say, "Praise God!" God has been so faithful throughout the past nine days. Without His strength holding me up, I would not have handled this accident very well. I look at my baby girl lying there and would do anything to take her pain away. A mother's love (and a father's, too) is deeper than anyone can imagine.

Mary Beth and I were talking about how God, the Most High Father of all, allowed His Son to come to earth. He could have sent anything, or anyone, to do the job. Barb was right when she wrote in her journal about how God gave the ultimate gift—His Son, so that we may have eternal life. Through that sacrifice we can see and feel the extent of God's love for each of us. I'm so excited to see that Ashley can breathe on her own. Even if it was just an hour, it's given me confidence that she'll be able to do it long term.

11:05 p.m.

I am encouraged by what's happened today. Not only did Ashley breathe on her own for one C-Pap test, she did it a second time for two hours. She did so well! The nurses are amazed at how much progress she has made over the past several days. They, too, thought the prognosis was dim, and her chances of survival remote. Like Mary Beth has been sharing with me, they are not looking at Ashley through God's eyes. I give all the glory to God and the power of prayer. We are witnessing a miracle of God's healing power. Ashley's drain tube was taken out today. They're talking about taking her off the ventilator tomorrow!

I had a chance to talk with a close friend tonight about God and His purpose in this whole thing. I think she was a little surprised to hear me thanking God and praising His name. If this accident brings people to Christ, I am willing to walk the path God has placed before us. We are overwhelmed by the people who have been touched by our daughter and her accident. It took us a long time to open the many cards and letters that we received in just the last three days from people we know, and from those we don't— Christian brothers and sisters that are sharing our burden with us. Some of the most touching letters and cards are from strangers who just want to say how much Ashley has touched their lives, and how much they are praying for her.

Thursday, May 18, 2000
8:30 a.m.

> *I opened my eyes this morning, and I felt God's presence surrounding us. God is awesome! He has been faithful through every drop of rain in this storm. I feel Him calming the seas like He did in the Bible, and leading us through the storm by His mercy and grace.*

11:30 p.m.

> *Today was a roller-coaster ride. It started way up as I said in my 8:30 entry. I hit bottom around 3:30 this afternoon and not only have I recovered, but I'm sitting on top of the mountain. They took Ashley's ventilator tube out this afternoon. She had a rough time with it. Unfortunately, I walked into the room at the worst possible moment. For a few minutes, they thought they would have to do a tracheotomy. To make a long story short, Ashley didn't need it, and she is now breathing on her own. Thank You, God!*

> *I was very fearful today, yet I know the Bible tells us not to be. I need to remember there is nothing I can do for my little girl that God couldn't do in an instant. My devotion today was how prayer is the breath of life. It couldn't have been a timelier message with the doctors taking Ashley off the ventilator today. The power of prayer is enormous.*

Friday, May 19, 2000
9:20 a.m.

> *It has been eighteen hours, and Ashley is still breathing on her own. Her nurse said she had a really good night. Her breathing is controlled at a normal pace along with her heart rate and blood pressure. It was really good to see my little girl this morning. The nurses washed her hair for the first time. She has two ponytails. God is so good.*
>
> *I was encouraged after meeting with the rehabilitation doctors. Dr. Ramor is known for making great strides with brain injury patients. Ashley's injury to the pones area of her brain is a little uncommon, however, and the doctor said that area is where automatic behaviors occur (breathing, heart rate, etc.). Thankfully, Ashley is doing pretty well in those areas. I'm hoping rehab starts the beginning of the week.*

8:30 p.m.

> *The day ended once again after another wild roller-coaster ride. The steps forward are much easier to deal with. It's the rocky road that sends my heart rate and anxiety levels haywire. The doctor moved all of Ashley's IV lines, fearing infection. He had some difficulty with the main line, but all is fine now.*

Saturday, May 20, 2000
6:30 p.m.

> *I spent the night at home last night for the first time since the accident. It felt good to be with my boys—Andrew and Michael. I also had a chance to share a*

little bit with some of the neighbors about God and his marvelous work in this whole thing. We serve a BIG God. I thank Him each day for where we are and the strength He provides.

Once I awoke, I was anxious to get back to the hospital. My baby girl looked so good. The respirator is out, her hair is in ponytails, and she is holding her little bun-bun. It's tough for Joe and me to remember the little girl she used to be. She really was, and is, the most precious little girl ever. We need to keep focused on God and know He is still in control, and know this is the plan He has for our family and not allow the past to overshadow our hope. I continue seeing, hearing, and sharing all the good things that God is doing through Ashley.

Joe and I read through the stack of good deeds that were done in Ashley's honor. Tears streamed down our cheeks as we read them.

Our Sunday school class planted pink flowers in all our flowerbeds at home.

8:30 p.m.

I've spent the last couple hours alone with Ashley and God. I read an article about how to survive the storms of life. God has revealed a lot about Himself and His purpose to me through the article. When you are in the midst of a storm, it's important to ask several questions:

- *What does God want to accomplish in this situation?*

- *What fruit does God want to produce in me?*

- *What does God want to reveal about Himself?*

- *How can He use my trials for someone else's benefit?*

God truly is using Ashley to draw both Joe and me closer to Him. He is also touching the hearts and souls of moms and dads across the country. God is faithful, and I truly believe He has a plan for each of us. Through this, I've already learned such compassion for others. It's been a humbling experience, and I've learned to depend fully on Him. He will give us what we need each day. God is my Shield, my Rock, my Strength, and is truly the God of all Comfort. God does not always shield us from the pain that comes from storms in our life, but He is there to pick up the pieces and grow us. Our pain is not in vain. God will use it for good just as He promises in Romans 8:28 for all those that love Him, and are called according to His purpose.

Sunday, May 21, 2000
9:30 p.m.

Ashley had a pretty long day. She awoke around 6:00 a.m. and with the exception of a little catnap has been awake most of the day. Right now her heart rate is up, and she is having difficulty falling asleep. There are classical lullabies playing softly in the background. I pray God covers her with His peace so she might be able to soon fall asleep. It breaks my heart to see her so restless as she lies in her bed. It's as if she is trapped inside that little body and wants so desperately to talk, yell, or cry. I cannot wait for the day she and I get into a battle over what she wants to wear, or about what cup she drinks from. Of course, I will win the battle, but it sure will be great to hear her little voice.

They finally gave her some Adivan to help her settle down. It seems to have worked because she's finally dozing off. I love my little girl so much and pray to God for a complete recovery. We do not know how this story will end but God does. This is where trust comes in. She's already a miracle in the making. I hope she continues to improve for a long time. I know God is holding her little body and is healing it the way He sees fit. I praise God for all He has done.

Week Three

Monday, May 22, 2000
10:10 a.m.

Ashley had a restless night. Debbie came and got me up around 3:30 a.m. I'm glad she did because I was able to get Ashley calmed down. We took little catnaps together throughout the morning. All things look like a go for rehab tomorrow.

The most exciting moment of the day was when Ashley sat up on her own (with the help of several nurses) for a few seconds. Her little body was like a bowl of Jell-O. It was difficult to see her unable to use any of her muscles. The doctors said that her brain has been completely erased. She has fewer skills than a newborn baby. I never realized just how much the brain controls your body's functions. Your body may be physically able to do something, but if your brain doesn't tell your lungs to breathe, or your heart to pump, or your hand to raise, or your throat to swallow, or your vocal cords to talk or cry, it doesn't get done.

11:00 p.m.

When I fell into my bed, I was once again overwhelmed with emotion. Ashley continues to make slow progress. Emotionally, this has been a really tough day for me. I just want my little girl back! I went home to put the boys in bed. It was good to be with them for a short time. I love my family and wish we could all be together again.

Tuesday, May 23, 2000
9:30 p.m.

Wow! What a day! Ashley is now sound asleep in her new bed on the third floor. It was a really, really big day. I am so grateful to God that He has brought us this far. He has made a miracle happen in Ashley already, and my guess is that He is not done yet. In just two weeks, He has brought her from that awful night when the doctors didn't think she would survive, to tonight where she is sleeping peacefully. There were once nine different machines and monitors hooked to her, and now there is nothing.

We really do serve an awesome God. Pastor Heath shared with me yesterday that wondering what lies ahead is not necessarily doubting or worrying.

The Bible says do not worry about anything. I guess there is a fine line between worrying and wondering. I have faith that God is going to heal Ashley in the way that is best for her and our family. It's when we are obedient to God and truly trust Him to heal according to His will that we receive the strength, joy, and peace of being free from worry. Sure, I wonder where she will be in ten years, but I don't worry about it. It's all in the hands of a sovereign God.

When they first moved Ashley to the rehab floor, they put her in with the ventilator babies. The environment, where monitors went off every couple minutes for one reason or another, was chaotic. Each alarm, although it was not for Ashley, made my heart race. I was looking forward to getting away from all that.

My mom and sister were with me and encouraged me to ask if there was another room. God also prompted me to be bold. In confidence, I asked if Ashley could be moved to another room. The only other bed available was in a room with a 78-year-old lady, Dottie Heagy. She and Ashley had had their accidents on the same day. They asked Dottie if it would be all right to put Ashley in her room.

"*I don't care if she doesn't care,*" *Dottie said.*

I think this will be a great situation. Dottie seems full of life. She really enjoys Ashley and the company our family brings to the room.

11:30 p.m.

Shirley came over tonight to sit with Ashley. I forgot to call and tell her she didn't need to come because I can now sleep beside Ashley's bed. But I'm glad she came because I really enjoyed her visit. I had a chance to run upstairs and check my e-mail. I couldn't believe how many people have been writing (I need to improve my typing skills so I can e-mail back quicker). When I got back downstairs, we had some time to sit and talk. We did our devotions together. Mine was on being more Christ-like. The bottom line is we are human, and we are going to fail, but God doesn't let go of us because we don't exhibit Christ-like behavior in a certain situation.

Shirley's devotion was on loving God with all your heart, all your soul, and all your mind. Spending time with God is so important. He truly desires a relationship with us. It's in that relationship that He can speak to us and strengthen us for our trials. I am glad I have a personal relationship with God. I have always known about Him. But I can say in all honesty that only recently have I begun to realize what the key to true life is—having a personal relationship with Jesus Christ, our Lord and Savior.

Thursday, May 25, 2000
10:15 p.m.

It has been two days since I've written in my journal. When I finally had a chance last night it was midnight, and I didn't have the energy to pick up my pen.

Ashley had her first full day of rehab today. They said it was going to be completely different and very busy down on the third floor, and they were right. Ashley has two to three hours of rehab in the morning, and then another two to three hours in the afternoon. They really work her hard. It's amazing that for one, the brain does so much, and for another, that these therapists actually know how to retrain it. I am impressed with the complete care we have received here at Hershey Medical Center. Everyone from the doctors to nurses to therapists to volunteer staff has been wonderful. I sincerely feel God is working through each of them to perform a miracle in our little girl.

Joe and I are continually overwhelmed by the love and support shown us. I now understand fully what Barb meant when she said the love and support is overwhelming. I feel very blessed to have family and friends who love us so very much. I think my mom is on the top of the list. She has been right by my side through this. (If you are reading my journal, Mom, thanks for being a great mom.)

Another thing that is overwhelming is the amount and extent of good deeds that are being done in honor of Ashley. Tears bubble up every time I read one of the many good deeds that have been done in her name.

One card that came in today was from a lady who paid the grocery bill of an elderly lady who was standing in front of her at the grocery store. She went on to tell the older woman how Ashley, a four-year-old little girl she didn't even know, had touched her life. She was also

God's Grace: Not an Easy Promise

moved by how we turned tragedy into triumph. (It really is not our turning this situation into triumph, but God and only God.)

Another card explained that many potted sunflowers were passed out at a workplace. The pots of flowers were named "Ashley's Sunshine" and would be planted outside in her name. The list of good deeds goes on and on.

We have even received two thank-you notes from people who have received a good deed done for them in Ashley's honor.

God is always at work around us. I learned that in my Bible study and believe it is true. All the events and stories connected to Ashley's accident are the clearest example of God's work that I have ever seen. He is working in the hearts and lives of so many people. He has shown me the true power of prayer as He continues to work a miracle in our little girl. Joe and I often said God had a big plan for our oldest son's life. He is extra kind and gentle. We did not know, however, the enormous work He had for Ashley. Maybe Andrew's big assignment is just to be Ashley's big brother.

I pray God continues to work through our family to bring all glory and honor to His name. Second Corinthians 12:10 says we must delight ourselves in hardships, weaknesses, insults, persecutions, and difficulties. When I first came across this passage at the beginning of my storm, I couldn't understand it. I wondered how you could do that—delight in hardships like this one? The passage goes on to say for when I am weak, then I am strong. God has equipped Joe and me with what we need to stay afloat as the seas rage beneath us. It is in His hands I am able to get through each day. His grace is sufficient to carry me through and make me strong. It's when I feel completely broken, and I have cried all the tears I have left that the Lord strengthens me. It's going to be an extremely long haul for Ashley and our family, but with God, we are up for the challenge.

While I sit and write in my journal, Ashley is sound asleep in the bed next to me. We gave her a bath tonight and washed her hair. I stood and combed her beautiful hair, and I felt such gratitude to the Lord for saving her life. I could not imagine my life, or Joe's, or Andrew's, or Michael's, without her. I stand firm on my faith that God is going to heal her totally. It might take a long time for her to come back, but I feel as if she will. I need to concentrate on how far we've come and not on how far we have to go.

I've written a lot in my journal tonight. But before turning in for the night, I thought I would read from my devotional for today—May 25. It absolutely amazes me how God knew these devotions, written months ago for publication, are exactly what I need.

For example, last Thursday, the day Ashley was removed from the ventilator, the big issue was whether or not she could breathe on her own. The devotion for that day was on prayer and how prayer is the breath of life. Without it, our Christian life turns blue.

Tonight the devotion I turned to was about patience; how patience is waiting without worrying. The footnotes in my Bible for the cited Scripture (Isaiah 40:27-31) says even the strongest people get tired at times but God's power and strength never diminishes.

When you feel all of life crushing you, and you feel you cannot go another step, remember you can call upon God to renew your strength. The devotion also says that if we hope in the Lord (expect His promise of strength) and trust in God to speak to us, we can be patient when He asks us to wait. Those who are patient will soar on wings like eagles. They will run and not grow weary; they will walk and not be faint. I must remember to hope and trust in God as we wait patiently for Ashley to walk again.

Friday, May 26, 2000
10:30 p.m.

Ashley is finished with her therapy for the week. She's had three sessions to date, and I can already see her progress. It's amazing to me that the brain is retrainable. Rob, Laurie, and Jen are the best! It's comforting to know that Ashley is in the very best place she can be.

The physical therapists have had lots of good results with brain injury recovery. Ashley's brain is repairing itself at this very moment. She is sound asleep. She had a big day, and we were able to get outside for a little walk with my mom. The sunshine and fresh air felt good. I'm sure it had to feel good to Ashley, too.

> Ashley's nurse tonight is kind. She taught me how to care for Ashley's neck brace. The collar isn't allowed to come off for twelve weeks, so I guess she'll be going home with it. We are eighteen days into her recovery. She's made great improvements so far. I wonder how she'll be in eighteen months.
>
> Our family is surviving. We have good days and bad ones. Joe and I have never been closer. We are both anxiously awaiting the day we can take Ashley home. Our family will be together again soon.

Saturday, May 27, 2000
11:00 p.m.

> It's been another good day for Ashley. She is beginning to show progress. Her right hand is becoming more purposeful. I'm delighted to see the little improvements with every passing day.
>
> Andrew and Michael came to the hospital today. Michael is such a little card; he cracks us up with the funny things he does. Andrew has been quieter lately. I see him looking at his sister with lots of questions stirring around in his head. Joe and I worry because he doesn't talk about things.
>
> We went to Friendly's for dinner tonight with the boys. It felt odd asking for a table for four. I really missed Ashley's presence. It won't be long before we're a group of five again. By the end of the night, Andrew seemed more like himself. Joy spent the evening with Ashley, and Joe and I went home with the boys.

Andrew really needed that. He's excited that we will get him bunk beds for his room. It'll be good for the two boys to be together.

Kristen, an old babysitter from college who was home for the summer, e-mailed and asked if we needed someone to care for the boys. She said she could come back and stay with them over the summer. What a God-thing! Joe and I felt the need for someone to be with the boys on a consistent basis. Our God is so good.

Sunday, May 28, 2000
10:00 p.m.

Wow! What a big, big day. It started off in such a beautiful way. Joe and I went to Sunday school. It was wonderful to be with so many people who really care for us and share our love for the Lord. God gave me exactly what I needed to share with everyone.

While praying one night, God told me to get up and write some things for Sunday school the following morning. The only paper I could find was Barb's journal pages.

We had a great time of sharing in Sunday school, and then Hal Royer spent a few minutes giving the lesson. He's teaching on the Beatitudes. The one for today was from Matt. 5:3, "Blessed are the poor in spirit, for theirs is the kingdom of heaven." The poor in spirit are those who know that without Christ we are nothing. Money and power are not important. It's faithful obedience from our hearts that enables us to be part of the kingdom of heaven.

Ashley's accident has certainly humbled us. We are poor in spirit. Without God, we couldn't survive this storm. "You are so strong," people said. It's only by the grace of God that we maintain our strength. This is something neither Joe nor I would be able to handle on our own. Our family and friends have been so supportive. I pray each night that God continues to use this situation to glorify His name. If we are obedient to God and allow Him to use us to do His work, He will certainly take care of all the details. He has already blessed us in such a big way—we still have our little princess.

Ashley had lots of visitors today. Grandma was here, of course, and then Tim and Sharon came, Carol and Tommy, Debbie, Fannie and Gus, Mina and Rob, Sharon and Amanda, and Brad and Lee. We are all very encouraged by Ashley's progress.

This journal has been therapeutic for me. It's given me a chance to reflect and record all that God has revealed about Himself, His purposes and His ways. I am grateful for His love and His everyday miracles. I'm grateful, not only for Ashley's progress, but how He is working in so many hearts and souls of people we know and even people we don't know. All this because of what happened to one little four-year-old girl. I want to make a banner to hang over Ashley's bed that says, "God's not finished with me yet!"

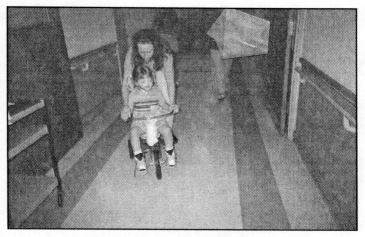

The therapists waisted little time getting Ashley on a bicycle again.

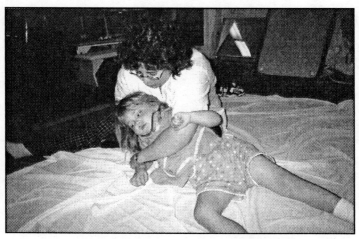

Learning to roll over again was a difficult task.

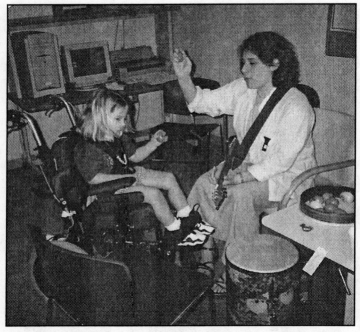

Ashley seemed to enjoy her time with the music therapist.

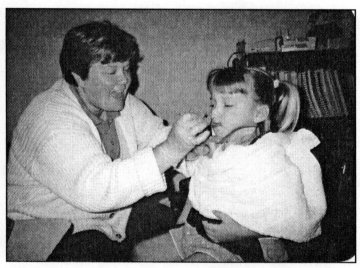

It took Ashley six weeks to learn how to swallow again.

Week Four

Tuesday. May 29, 2000
11:00 p.m.

It's hard for me to find time to write in my journal during the day. Ashley is so busy from the time she wakes up in the morning until 3:45 in the afternoon. After a few visitors come in the evening, it's not long before we get into the bedtime routine.

Ashley worked really hard in therapy today. I'm excited about the little things we see each day. She moved her right hand and leg in response to stimuli. This was the first time we really saw a specific move. The therapists really like her upper body control and the fact she can put weight on her legs when being balanced.

I'm impressed with Rob, Jen, and Laurie. They played a major role in Ashley's recovery. Joy was here with her tonight and gave her a good bath and massage. Ashley went to sleep at 10:00.

It's only 11:00 now but Ashley is already awake and somewhat agitated. The doctors say this phase will get worse as she continues to recover from her brain injury. It's tough to see her like this. As a mother, I want to comfort her and make her comfortable. Unfortunately, I agree with the doctor, I think it's going to get worse before it gets better.

I spent some time with Michael and Andrew tonight. God has truly blessed our family. They seem to be doing OK with the way things are. Time will pass quickly enough, and soon we will be together as a family again.

Wednesday, May 30, 2000
11:00 p.m.

Well, here I sit again late at night with a pen in hand. As tired as I am, I'm excited about what God is doing, and I couldn't go to bed without writing in this journal.

Deb Stein and Shirley visited us tonight. We gave Ashley a bubble bath and got her ready for bed. The three of us then sat and shared what has happened as a result of Ashley's accident.

"I had been praying for our neighbors to come to know God in a closer way," Deb said softly.

Deb had been praying for three families. The hours immediately following the accident gave her a divinely appointed opportunity to pray with one of our neighbors who desired a life with God and had been searching. In fact, the woman had talked with Deb several times about it. Faithfully, Deb prayed for that neighbor.

I, too, prayed for a long time that God would draw Joe closer to Him. Although Joe has been a Christian for a long time, I felt he was missing that whole bit about relationship. The closer I draw to God, the more I desire for my husband to grow close to Him, also.

Although Deb and I had been praying for something to draw others close to God, I don't feel He arranged for Ashley to fall off her bike that night because we had been praying. I do think God used the situation to make us stronger and to reveal Himself to us. God desires a love relationship with each one of us; He wants that relationship to be real and personal.

I really enjoyed spending time with Shirley and Deb. After they left, I had an opportunity to talk with two different nurses about God: one was a man who lives close to my sister. We talked about how much we love the Lord.

The other nurse, a member of our church, said, "I love the pink ribbons that have been placed all around town." It is amazing to see the love, support, and prayers that people are offering daily on behalf of Ashley and our family. We are fortunate that so many people love us.

My nurse friend also mentioned a friend who had a similar brain injury. "Her injury required several surgeries to stop the swelling and bleeding," she said. "My friend has made a remarkable recovery, and she now walks and talks like normal."

That information was highly encouraging. I look at all the wonderful things Ashley has accomplished and think of all the prayers that are being offered daily, and I know God will heal Ashley to the fullest extent that is best for her, and for us. We will take her any way God allows. I'm encouraged tonight to think she might have a major recovery. I pray so.

Friday, June 2, 2000
9:45 p.m.

I look at Ashley tonight; sound asleep in her hospital pj's, and I think how fortunate we are to still have her. The nurse gave her a bath tonight, and I washed her hair. Joe came to the hospital right on time and was able to read her a story before she faded off to sleep. I love this little girl with all my heart. If she thought I hugged and kissed her a lot before the accident, just wait until I get her home!

I read today's devotional with Joe and once again it seemed as if God wrote it especially for us. It said Jesus is our Rock when storms strike. This storm struck when we were unprepared; thunder raged and lightning pierced the sky when we weren't looking. I don't know of any stronger storm that we've ever been in. I thank God for solid ground— Jesus, our Rock.

I find that I talk to God often throughout the day. I know God can heal Ashley instantly. My cousin, Annie, brought me a little card that says, "Now faith is being sure of what we hope for and certain of what we do not see." We cannot see our future, only God can. My faith reassures me that God is sovereign and will take care of all my tomorrows. He knows my heart and my desires, and what is the very best for me. It's all about trust.

God's Grace: Not an Easy Promise

Saturday, June 3, 2000
1:30 p.m.

Happy birthday, Michael! It's hard to believe two years ago I was in labor with my little boy at the other end of the third floor in the maternity ward of this very same hospital.

I had a pretty rough morning. Waking up each day and seeing my little daughter lying in a hospital bed can be tough. Today was especially difficult because it's Michael's birthday.

Michael's birthday. Joe, I, and the three kids normally would be snuggling in our queen-size bed, watching Saturday morning cartoons and laughing hysterically. Joe would be tickling Michael's tummy, and saying, "Happy birthday, Michael!" Michael would start laughing, and all of us would erupt in laughter.

I punched the numbers on the hospital phone, and waited until I heard my husband's cheery voice. "J-Joe," I said. "This is really hard . . ." I wiped the tears sliding down my face.

"Can we change anything that's happened, Rose?" he asked.

"No."

"Then, we can only do the very best we can with today."

God's Grace: Not an Easy Promise

Joe seems to be strongest when I'm really disheartened, and when he's down I'm usually up. I guess that's what makes us such strong soul mates. God has certainly blessed our marriage through this tragedy.

We had a little birthday party for Michael in the dining room here at the hospital. It was good for our family to be together. Andrew wanted to sit beside Ashley in her wheelchair.

At one point, I saw Andrew reach down and grab his sister's hand. It was a Kodak moment, and I took a picture of them holding hands. What a beautiful expression of love.

I don't want to go home. I know I need a break from the hospital, but it is so hard to be home without my Ashley.

From the depths of my soul, I cried out to the Lord. "My body is weary, and my heart is aching, Lord." I feel so broken before Him. I try to remind myself that only God can restore our baby girl. It's been such a long road.

I eventually decided to go home. Later that evening, I stood alone in Ashley's bedroom and looked around. I felt comforted that she would be coming home soon to her own bed and toys. I love my little girl so much, but I know God loves her even more.

When I spoke to Joe earlier in the day, he said something that rang true.

> "We wouldn't have chosen this for our lives, but we were chosen for it," he said. That reminds me of what Patty said in a letter—God uses the obedient for His work. He knew I would give Him my all. When He commissions a believer to do His work, He equips them with everything they need to accomplish His good deeds. I believe that with all my heart. It is through Him I receive the strength I need to carry on and the words I need to share with others so I can bring Him glory.

Sunday, June 4, 2000
11:15 p.m.

> Ashley had such a good day! From the time I got to the hospital from Sunday school, I noticed she seemed really "with it." I held her on my lap and read her favorite books.
>
> That afternoon, she surprised me by moving her right leg. Later, when Vickie and Terry visited, she moved her leg in a very major way. She raised it up and crossed it over her left leg. Then she lifted it up, moved it halfway down, and then raised it again.
>
> "Next time it will be her arm," said Vickie. I looked hopelessly at Ashley's limp little body and thought, Yeah, but when? Two minutes later, she moved her arm! I can't wait to tell the doctors and her therapists tomorrow.
>
> Today has been as good as yesterday was bad. Again, I feel God strengthening me.

Sunday school blessed me today. My good faith friend, Barb Malinich, said that God had prompted her to tell me this was just a testing; a waiting time in my life, and that there are big plans that lie ahead.

God has brought Ashley through this life or death situation. It's now that waiting for her to improve gets longer and harder. I need to receive my strength from God and from people He puts in my path. I feel God used Barb to remind me of this test.

How will I stand in this storm? I was really discouraged yesterday and needed that reminder today. I'm ready to do God's work in any way I can. Four more weeks is a long time, but it will come and go before I know it, especially if I rely on my heavenly Father to help me. Days like today make it easier to look toward tomorrow.

Ashley is sleeping peacefully at the moment, but seems to have passing phases of agitation. I can only believe this is good. She's continuing to work through the phases of brain injury recovery. Praise God!

Week five

Monday, June 5, 2000
10:00 p.m.

Ashley had a bubble bath and her hair fixed, and she is now sleeping peacefully. When she's sleeping, she looks so much like the Ashley before the accident (except for her neck brace) that it's hard to believe she has lost all of her muscle tone and ability to do anything on her own. She has so much recovering to do.

Through it all, we feel blessed to have the support of family and friends. So many people say we are strong, but really we are nothing without God's grace. When you have a sick child, regardless of the illness, I believe God gives you the strength to do what needs to be done to help them get better.

I had a nice conversation with Mom about this today.

"Well, Rose," she said, "look at it this way, at least you're taking care of Ashley knowing she is getting better with each passing day; but when I took care of Barb, she was only getting sicker."

This gave me encouragement, but also made me feel a little sad for Mom. As a mother, that must have been the worst thing to experience—watching your child slip away from you. But God's grace was sufficient for my mom when she needed it the most. She took care of my sister each day and never complained that it was too tough or that she just couldn't do it anymore. My mom has been through many, many storms in her lifetime, and God seems to bring her out of each one a little bit stronger than before.

We kid her and say she's a "tough old bird," but she's really one of the strongest, most compassionate, and *giving people I know. She taught every one of us not to give up when times get tough. I really admire my mom and hope that some day Ashley looks up to me the same way I look up to my mother.*

Ashley's roommate, Dottie, was finally able to go home. We sure will miss our adopted grandmother, but I know our relationship will continue once Ashley gets out of here.

Ashley's new roommate was in a soccer accident the same weekend Ashley had her accident. Lindsey spent the first four weeks at Lancaster General. She was moved here today.

I find it interesting that Lindsey and Ashley are roommates since they have similar head injuries. Lindsey is able to move her arms and legs, plus she's able to swallow. She does, however, have a tracheotomy. The girls will be roommates for at least the next four weeks. It's hard to believe that riding a bicycle or playing soccer can cause this much damage to a body. We can protect our children the best we know how, but accidents happen in a split second.

All the pieces of Ashley's accident came together in such a strange way, and it helps me see that what happened was truly a freak accident. God did not cause the accident to happen but chose to use what happened for His glory. I know He will give us the strength to get through each day. My thought for today is God answers our prayers, one day at a time.

Tuesday, June 6, 2000
11:00 p.m.

This will be a short entry tonight because I am exhausted.

Ashley had a very good day today. I asked that they not give her the medicine for agitation last night. She slept pretty well without it, and then was wide-awake in the morning. Her glazed-over look had almost disappeared; she looked much better.

Personally, I think the medicine was giving her a hangover every morning, which lasted well into the day. I'm glad I realized what was happening. Her therapists also commented on how bright she looked.

As a parent of a sick child, I think it's important to be aware of what's going on medically with your child and be their strongest advocate.

Wednesday, June 7, 2000
10:35 p.m.

Another good day for Ashley! Her eyes seem to be tracking. I'm so excited about this occurrence because it makes me think my little girl might have a chance to see pink—her favorite color—again some day. I sure hope so.

The cards and letters people send are uplifting. I received one from a good friend, Laura Neece, which really cheered me.

"I feel that the year 2000 will be a special year to experience the presence of Jesus, and that He will meet us in our suffering," she wrote. For me, I have to say I certainly can attest to that. Barb's journey home to be with the Lord and Ashley's accident have opened up opportunities for me to experience God firsthand. Not only have I seen God clearly, but I've had the chance to share Him with so many others.

In the past, I've prayed over and over that God would use my family and me to do His work here on earth. I have always felt more than blessed and have been so grateful to God for all He has given me. I sit here now, and I watch my sweet little girl's chest gently rising and falling with each breath, and I feel that God took me up on my offer to use my family to reach others.

Amazingly, my little girl has touched so many people. People are sharing our burdens as they lift my Ashley up in prayer every day. Thank you, God, for your goodness.

Thursday, June 8, 2000
11:20 p.m.

It's raining tonight, and I sit down once more to write in my journal. As the rain slides down the window, I feel an overwhelming sense of love and support from friends, family, and God Himself. When I feel discouraged, God always seems to send something or someone to pick me up: an encouraging note, just the right devotion for the day, a visit from a friend, or a new movement from

Ashley. God knows all our needs. I'm learning that He will give us exactly what we need for each day. It's when we realize He won't give us any less or any more of what we need that we can rest in His presence throughout the day—no matter what happens.

In fact, He turned a potentially discouraging day into a really OK day for me. Ashley slept a lot today and instead of feeling at ease over her ability to rest, I worried (typical mom, huh?). By lunchtime, I was completely disheartened. I even buried my head in my pillow and sobbed. I felt sorry for myself and though I probably had the right to throw a pity party, it got me nowhere.

But my day turned around. A special friend met me for lunch. Then my mother arrived, and I received the Elizabethtown Chronicle that had Ashley's picture and story on the front page.

The day ended with some very special time with Mary Beth, and some time with my husband. Later that day, Ashley's right foot and leg moved quite a bit, and she rolled over on her side all by herself. My day is certainly ending better than it began.

Many people say inspirational things to me. I try to make mental notes or write down thoughts so I won't forget how God speaks to me through other people. One thing I do remember is someone saying how God uses ordinary people to do extraordinary work. We are certainly ordinary people; there's nothing special about my family. I become excited when I think God can use us for extraordinary things.

Someone else said there's a fine line between reality and faith. It comforts me to know that with God all things are possible.

Mary Beth and I talked about so many interesting things tonight. I could sit and talk with her all night. She has been a great mentor to me on my Christian walk.

"God's planning is perfect," she said. "You know, He prepares us and equips us for what lies ahead." I am so thankful to know that God loves Ashley more than we do, and He has the perfect life planned for her. He is really big, and He has everything under control.

I read the article about Ashley in the newspaper five or six times. Her picture is striking . . . so beautiful. The article was nicely written.

After Ashley's company was gone for the night, and Ashley slept, I flipped through the rest of the newspaper. To my surprise, I found a second article written in the editorial section of the paper. This time the article was about me.

It spoke of my courage being at Ashley's bedside every day and my continued hope and faith in Ashley's recovery. The article expounded on my thinking of others instead of myself, and how that impacted the community.

It really touched me to find and read this second story in the newspaper. I certainly don't feel courageous except that I know God is beside me and will help me carry out His will and purpose. Any credit should be given to God.

Friday, June 9, 2000
10:15 p.m.

Ashley is doing some really nice stuff! She looked at a picture today, tracking it up and down the page. I'm excited about that. The doctors told us she would be completely blind, and yet I think God is telling us something different. She is really tugging and playing with things: her collar, her ears, her blanket, and her pajama buttons. She can roll pretty well with just the slightest initiation. Deb and Don were here and couldn't believe how good she looked. They said she seemed alert. I'm really encouraged by her progress so far. We have been very blessed with her life and her recovery.

Saturday, June 10, 2000
4:15 p.m.

Cindy Morris, a friend from church, started a sticker chart for Ashley, and every day she improves she receives another sticker. I'm thrilled to put sticker number thirty-three on the chart. It's been a quiet day.

Ashley had some therapy today and just one visitor. Chuck Grenauer came to visit. After a pleasant visit, Ashley (in her wheelchair) and I rode the elevator with him to the first floor. The gift shop was in my path, and I just couldn't resist going inside. I found a $20 bill in my back pocket though I couldn't remember how it got there, and I bought a book called Everyday Angels. As I travel on this journey, I find angels are intriguing.

God's Grace: Not an Easy Promise

My brother, Brad, gave me an angel that I carry in my pocket. Each time I reach into my pocket, I feel the smooth coin-like object with an angel molded into it, and I think about Ashley and all the angels who are watching over her. In fact, I am comforted knowing the Bible says in Matthew 18:10 that "their angels in heaven always see the face of my Father in heaven."

Mom wrote in Ashley's inspirational book that she felt Barb was Ashley's very own angel and was watching over her. I do believe we all have guardian angels protecting us and looking out for us every day.

This new book I bought Ashley says that each of us are angels deep inside our hearts as we daily help each other through acts of kindness.

After we left the gift shop, I pushed Ashley down the hall. Then I spied the hospital sanctuary. God prompted me to go in. Sitting in a front pew, I looked at my daughter and began singing, "Jesus Loves Me." Soon a nearby couple joined the singing. It was such a peaceful moment. I know with my whole heart that Jesus loves her and is taking care of her.

Sunday, June 11, 2000
11:00 p.m.

Once again, Ashley is moving into the agitation phase of the brain recovery. She often gets upset and flails her left arm and leg. The nurses have padded her bed rails to protect her. She seems to get really agitated if she is too stimulated. But right now, she is sound asleep. I hope she can make it peacefully through the night.

It was good being home with Joe and the kids last night. We are all anxious for Ashley to come home. I think we will see lots of progress once she is in familiar surroundings with her family. She has made great progress so far, but I know we'll see her move along in recovery by leaps and bounds once she's home in her little pink bed again.

It is truly astonishing the amount of prayers offered each day for Ashley. Her name has reached people all over the United States and China. People have been sincerely committed to praying to God, our heavenly Father, on Ashley's behalf. Isn't it neat to think that God hears every single prayer, big or small, every single day? He is an awesome God!

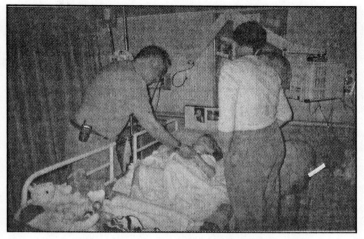

Tim and Sharon were two of the many who came to visit with Ashley.

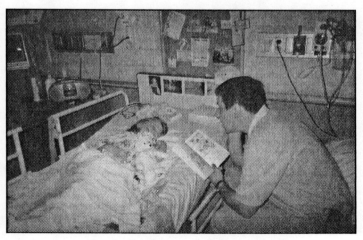

Daddy was her favorite visitor.

Mi-Mi holds Ashley after a long therapy session.

Cousin Amanda reads to Ashley.

Week Six

Tuesday, June 13, 2000
10:45 p.m.

Thirty-six days! Wow! It's really hard to believe it's been so long. Joe and I were talking tonight about the long-ago intensive care days. When we were living those days, they seemed to last forever. We thought the time would never pass but here we are, three weeks into rehab already with a lot of hope. As humans, we seem to be caught up in living in this world, and we are easily distracted from our main goal—getting to heaven. This world is not our home; we're just passing through.

I didn't get a chance to write in my journal last night, not because I didn't have anything to say, but because when this room finally settled, I didn't want to take a chance on disrupting it.

Ruth, Ashley's new 92-year-old roommate, had a tough night. She was in intense pain, more than she felt she could handle. When they finally got her settled for the night, she lay in her bed and prayed to God to let her die. It was sad to hear an elderly lady call upon the Lord to take her home. I sat and held her hand until a nurse relieved me.

I listened to Ruth, and I thought of another good friend who was just entering her own painful storm. She and her husband have grown in their faith over the past year. I hope they are able to receive strength from God to accept and deal with the obstacles that have burdened their lives.

God's Grace: Not an Easy Promise

When I read my devotional today, I turned to a page that had a passage underlined. It said, "God doesn't shield us from pain that comes with living in a fallen world, but He uses it to accomplish His loving purposes." No one can avoid the storms of life. When we realize God has a hand in everything that happens to us and that He is in control, we can rest assured that the storm will be used to bring glory to Him. His work is accomplished through us. The Scripture about the potter and the clay comes to mind. We are the clay that God molds and uses to complete His purposes, His will, and His ways. We need to be obedient and stay focused on Him to keep our storms from becoming even more violent than they already are.

Wednesday, June 14, 2000
9:45 p.m.

I'm overwhelmed by emotions again as I write in my journal tonight. It has been such a good day. Ashley went on her first outing from the hospital since the night she arrived five weeks ago. We went to Chocolate World for her therapy session. As a family, we have gone to Chocolate World many, many times. Her therapists wanted us to take her someplace familiar in the public arena to see how she would respond to lots of stimuli.

The van pulled up, and we wheeled her wheelchair into it, secured the belts and we were off. She did great! I believe I even saw her smile.

The other exciting thing that happened was she drank a little juice from a cup and ate an ounce of ice cream. We're pretty sure that she is swallowing even though we can't see her swallow because of the neck collar. The doctor has decided that it's time to push ahead with eating, which means we can soon have the feeding tube removed. It amazes me that it's taken thirty-seven days for her to relearn how to swallow.

Sharon and Amanda came to sit with Ashley tonight, and I went home for dinner. It was really nice to be home with Joe and the boys. I took Andrew to Bible school, and Joe took Michael to the circus with Tommy and Sherri. Michael doesn't get much one-on-one time with his daddy. I'm glad they went.

Bible school was great. The theme is called "Faith Island," which is a Hawaiian theme. Steven Courtney does a fantastic job leading it. The Bible verse for the night was 2 Corinthians 5:7, "We live by faith, not by sight." How true that is. It's ironic that Mary Beth wrote in Ashley's Inspirational Journal today about how important it is that we live each day by faith, knowing that God will take care of tomorrow. He is the one that knows and sees all. Living by faith means putting the fear behind you and resting easy in the knowledge that God is holding you tight.

Sometimes I feel as though my life is on pause. I miss being home and doing all the everyday "mom" things. I need to remember, however, that God makes no mistakes, and He knows exactly where I am. This is the path He chose for our lives. He has given Joe and me the strength and patience to persevere each day.

I get excited seeing the miracle God is performing in Ashley. I love the sign that hangs in her room here at the hospital. A neighbor made it for her and brought it in the other day. It reads, "God's not finished with me yet!" Along with those words are three Scripture verses, " . . . he who began a good work in you will carry it on to completion until the day of Christ Jesus" (Phil. 1:6b), "I can do all things through Christ who strengthens me" (Phil. 4:13, NKJV), and "I will love you, O Lord, my strength" (Psalm 18:1, NKJV). I pray each night that God uses the miracle He is performing in Ashley to reach out and change others.

Ashley has touched so many lives already. The letters we've received are wonderfully moving. Many of them tell how our little girl has altered the way they look at life. I think there have been a lot more hugs and kisses being given to children since May 8, 2000.

I get a kick out of my friend, Sonya, who says her kids run when they see Mom because they know she is going to grab them and hug them again. There have been so many lessons learned and lives changed that I see this tragedy evolving into triumph. Ashley's recovery truly is a miracle, and God is not finished with her yet.

It's hard to believe this is Wednesday already. The time is passing quickly. The kind nurses and therapists help the days go by faster. Ruth has turned out to be a pretty good roommate. It's really not a bad idea for a 92-year-old and a 4-year-old to room together. I think Ashley and our family are good for Ruth. She really is one of the sweetest ladies I have ever met. She shares the Holy Spirit with Ashley. Every morning she tells Ashley to say good morning to the Holy Spirit (even though Ashley cannot speak yet), and every night they say good night to the Holy Spirit.

Thursday, June 15, 2000
10:15 p.m.

Ashley continues to amaze me because she takes some new step every day on her road to recovery. God continues to teach me as well, inch by inch, as we journey down this road with Ashley. The lessons He teaches are life changing. I am learning how to find peace in the midst of chaos.

The most significant baby step Ashley took today was experimenting with her voice. I heard three little attempts at words early in the day, and then later at night. She became very vocal in her agitation phase.

I recall talking to my sister, Vickie, on the phone. She could not believe the background noise coming from Ashley. Vickie was so excited she put my brother-in-law on the phone. The thought of hearing my sweet little girl talk again is exciting. Her speech therapist said this is a normal stage of vocalization. It's called groping.

She thinks Ashley's voice and words are just around the corner. If tonight's noises are any indication of what she's planning to say, we better be prepared. I'm thankful her roommate has a hearing aid that she can remove. Ruth and Ashley are both sound asleep right now—the young and the old together. Each of them brings so much joy. I'm glad Ruth is Ashley's roommate. We all benefit from the relationship.

Friday, June 16, 2000
11:30 p.m.

As tired as I am, I cannot go to bed without recording the day's events. Ashley ate a container of yogurt for breakfast and lunch, and had some pudding for dinner. She will not open up her mouth for a big bite, but will work it around her teeth and mouth, and then swallow. I'm hoping the feeding tube will come out next week.

Ashley seemed extremely agitated tonight. I think we are really seeing some of her personality and temper reviving. It's tough physically and emotionally to watch her go through this stage of recovery, but I know it's common and a sign that she is getting better. I hope it passes quickly.

The hospital's chaplain came to see me tonight. He asked how I keep my energy level up. It's only through God's empowerment that I'm able to get through each day, both physically and mentally. When I get down, God always seems to lift me up. For when I am weak, then I am strong. The chaplain also said he thought my faith was an inspiration to many. The word "inspiration" has come up several times in the past week. Cindy Morris started an "Inspirations for Ashley" journal, the editorial in the *paper was called, "An inspiration for a small town," and the chaplain said my faith is an inspiration to many. I don't feel as if I am doing anything special. I'm just trying to obey God and carry out His will for the path He has laid ahead. I feel blessed that He is using ordinary people like my daughter and me to do His extraordinary work.*

Week Seven

Monday, June 19, 2000
11:05 p.m.

I didn't have a chance to write in my journal over the weekend. We were able to take Ashley on her first furlough home to see how things transpired. Caring for her in the home required a lot more energy than I realized. Not only did I have to be concerned with Ashley, but I also had the two boys and a mountain of housework.

In all honesty, however, I guess another reason for not writing was that I only wanted to write positive things in this journal. Having Ashley at home was much more difficult than I ever imagined. While living at the hospital for the last six weeks, I came up with a routine that worked for Ashley and me. But being away from the hospital disrupted my routine. The work I did for Ashley at home seemed a lot more exhausting.

Along with physical demands came the reality check of where Ashley is and how far she has yet to go. That's

God's Grace: Not an Easy Promise

when I got into big trouble. Instead of focusing on God and how far He has brought us, I was caught up in how far she has to go. When we fail to focus on God, our vision becomes blurred.

I opened a letter from a good friend, Melissa Gizzi, who talked about life being a one-way street. No matter how many detours you take, none of them leads back. You must accept that life becomes much simpler because you know you must do the best you can with what you have, and what you are, and what you have become.

There is no road that will lead us back to May 8. We need to accept where we are and continue forward. This accident has changed who we are and is having a big impact on who we become. I see it all as positive. When I got really discouraged, I put Ashley in the car and went for a drive. It amazes me and uplifts me to see all the pink ribbons tied around town reminding people to pray for my daughter.

Joe and I struggled to remain on track this weekend. After the accident, we realized that people deal with tragedy differently. We understood that and accepted it. I talked to my girlfriends, and Joe had his guy friends over to sit and watch a movie, and not talk. We each dealt with the situation in the best way we could.

Six weeks later, however, we are together again and the same issue of how to deal with the accident has resurfaced. I was glad we were able to talk about it in a semi- productive manner. Our discussion ended on a great note with both of us recommitting ourselves to each other and to God. Once again, I see how important it is to keep God in the forefront of all things and to stay focused on Him.

The best news of the day is that Ashley is moving her right leg—a lot. We had seen it move in the past, but nothing like today. Her arm is also moving more than before.

Tuesday, June 20, 2000
9:15 p.m.

Day forty-three of this ordeal ended early and on a good note. Ashley had her bath around 7:15, and by 8:15, everything was done and she went to sleep. She was less agitated tonight than the past few evenings. Maybe this is a sign that she is moving out of the agitation phase.

I was able to get her to bed earlier without too much commotion. She really needs her environment to be extremely quiet. She had such a great day. Her daddy was here with her for therapy. She did some pretty cool stuff. She is able to follow directions more each day.

Ashley's upper body control is increasing all the time. I am overjoyed when I see her progress. The new thing for the day is that we are beginning to see her tongue. Up to this point she has kept her teeth clenched together. She is even exploring her mouth, nose, ears, and hair with her finger.

God's Grace: Not an Easy Promise

Ashley finally has a good appetite. For dinner, she ate some chicken potpie, broccoli, peaches, pears, yogurt, and drank some Juicy Juice. Her eating has progressed since last week, and I'm looking forward to having the feeding tube removed. That will be the next big step in her recovery. I thank God and give Him all the glory for bringing us this far.

Wednesday, June 21, 2000
12:02 p.m.

I'm actually finding time each day to write in my journal—imagine that. I can't contain my excitement today. Ashley's feeding tube is out! They pulled it this morning. I'm so thankful to God. He truly is doing amazing work through this little girl. I hope she is able to become hydrated enough to keep it out.

I've been thinking a lot about everyday angels—people who seem to pop up with a cup of coffee and cheesecake (my friend, Marcie, last night), or send an encouraging note when I need it (my friend Melissa Gizzi), or just happen to stop in the room to offer a prayer of thanksgiving for the feeding tube being removed (the hospital pastor).

God has ordained all those acts of kindness, and people have willingly obeyed His calling, and become an everyday angel for me.

Many blessings come from God when we hear His voice and obey His commands. I truly believe my friend, Mary Beth, was sent from God to be my very best everyday angel here on earth.

> *Guardian angels watch over you.* Mom wrote in Ashley's inspirational book that she feels one of Barb's jobs in heaven is to be Ashley's very own guardian angel. I don't think God called her home for that reason, but I do feel strongly that she is watching over her little niece. There's so much about angels I don't know. I can't wait to get to heaven to find out more.

> Kim Reese was here today and talked about God's angels encamped around Ashley as she continues her journey to recovery. It's a great feeling to think of God's angels surrounding her and guarding her.

10:45 p.m.

> Sharon came to sit with Ashley while I went to my Bible study. I'm so glad I did because it was on attitude. As we make our way down the zigzag road of life, attitude is very important. Attitude is everything. We are to be Christ-like in our attitude to everyone, every day.

Thursday, June 22, 2000
9:05 p.m.

> The days seem to speed by. It's hard to believe tomorrow is Friday already. I'm trying to be quiet as Ashley falls asleep. There are so many outside noises that seem to arouse her. Hospital walls are thin. She was tired and ready for bed around 7:00, and it is now two hours later, and she's still awake. She has passed through the agitation phase, I think. She seems so much more peaceful than a week ago. It was hard seeing her like

that. Her arms and legs flailed, and she banged them on the bed rails. I'm surprised she didn't end up with lots of bruises. I remember asking the doctors and nurses if anyone ever got stuck in that phase of recovery.

11:00 p.m.

I'm tired, but I feel the need to write a few exciting things in my journal. Mary Beth was here for a few hours. We had such a great talk. It's really good having someone who will cry, laugh, shop, or just sit and talk with me for a couple of hours about the goodness of God.

"Ashley's almost through the agitation phase, Mary Beth."

My friend's eyes welled up with joy. "I'm sure that's an answer to our direct prayers to calm her agitation."

When Ashley was going through the agitation phase, I had asked for specific prayers for that and her vision. God knows our heart's desire to have her vision restored. Although we can't see the end result, we need to trust God and leave her vision in His hands. I submit Ashley and myself unto Him on a daily basis. God really is faithful.

As Mary Beth and I talked, I noticed my little girl sleeping peacefully. She didn't even need any medication to calm her.

In the quiet of the evening, Mary Beth and I talked about angels. She shared some of her encounters with

God-ordained everyday angels. I'm anxious to learn more about them. I think I should write a chapter on them in our book.

God gives us everything we need to complete a job when he commissions us to do His work. Take for instance the way He called me to step out in faith and write a book. I know nothing about writing a book, but at the same time I know God has called me to do it. I can hardly wait to see the end product. I have no idea what it's going to be like—but I know God already sees the finished product. He now calls me to trust and obey.

It's 11:30 p.m., and I'm more awake now than when I started writing in this journal. I get energized thinking about God's hand in all of this. I enjoy talking about it to other people. I believe that's our work as a Christian: to let our light shine and share His glorious name and good deeds with others.

Joe is out repairing an elevator tonight. We were supposed to have dinner together but instead he's with Chuck on a call. I just talked with him, and he said he thinks he found the problem. Amazingly, he just "happens" to have the right part in his truck to fix it. I reminded him there's no such thing as a coincidence, and things like that don't just happen. He needs to give God thanks for His help. Even though I had to remind him of God's grace, it does my heart good to know he was already aware and felt God's hand in it.

I'm very grateful to be married to a man who knows the Lord. Joe's faith has grown in great ways throughout the last forty-five days. It's good to know I will be with Joe forever, long after our days are through here on this earth. We will live together in heaven. Oh, what a glorious thought! Being reunited with our loved ones makes me anticipate heaven even more. I know Barb is waiting for us in the heavenly mansion Jesus has prepared for her. She will meet us at those pearly gates and what a wonderful reunion we will have.

Sunday, June 25, 2000
10:30 p.m.

People are so good. In this world, we often focus on the negative things that happen. Ashley's accident has truly shown us firsthand how much people care. We live in such a good Christian community. I feel as though many people are carrying our burden, and they want to help in any way possible. Prayers are the greatest things they can do for Ashley. I feel their prayers.

Ashley's vision doesn't seem to be improving. I know God hears each and every prayer, so I've been really encouraging people to pray specifically for that. In addition to prayers uplifted for Ashley, people have been encouraging Joe and me with their thoughtfulness and cards. There have been so many good deeds done in Ashley's honor.

I have often heard that a good deed is never lost. It comes back to the person who planted it through love and friendship. I'm glad good things are being done for others because of Ashley's accident. Wonderful things are also being done for Joe and me. People have been so kind. We have made some new friends and strengthened old friendships throughout the past seven weeks. These people are our everyday angels. God has definitely been faithful to our family. My favorite Bible verse showed up on a card today: Isaiah 40:31 says, "... but those who hope in the Lord will renew their strength. They will soar on wings like eagles; they will run and not grow weary, they will walk and not be faint."

The Lord renewed our strength when we felt as though we were at the end of our rope. I like to think that Ashley will soar on wings like eagles. God can give her the strength to walk and run, and not grow weary. Each day I put Ashley in His hands. His arms have been around her since the very beginning. God loves my little girl more than I do, which is a whole bunch. Joe and I will continue to wait on the Lord and try our best to stay focused on Him.

Ashley made such good progress last week. I'm really anxious to see what happens this week. God's not finished with her yet. I'm really thrilled to see my little girl's personality return. Maybe we will soon hear some words. It will be a great day when I hear Ashley say, "I love you, Mommy."

Week eight

Monday, June 26, 2000
7:30 p.m.

Wow! It's been exactly seven weeks tonight. It's really amazing that forty-nine days ago we didn't know if Ashley *would even make it through the night and here we are heading into our eighth week. She has come so far. Thank You, God! Today we got the official news that Ashley will be going home on Friday. Our family will be together again. Praise God!*

Ashley had a tough day in therapy today. She battled the therapists about everything. She wrinkled up her nose in defiance and pulled away. I couldn't believe how much of the old Ashley was coming to life. She really does get better each and every day.

A nurse said today that love and hope play such a major role in the recovery of these kids. I know for certain Joe and I have enough love and hope to give, but first and foremost, we have God in our corner, and He's holding Ashley's hand.

We are continually overwhelmed by the love and support given us. Today, a hospital volunteer delivered thirty-eight cards to Ashley's room. We were literally "showered" with cards from neighbors, friends, family, and strangers who wanted to lift our spirits. Hallmark has certainly sold some cards over the last forty-nine days. Each and every card means a great deal to us. God continues to bless my family. I am very grateful for all He has done.

Wednesday, June 28, 2000
11:10 p.m.

I didn't write in my journal yesterday for two reasons: one, I was tired, and two, I was a little depressed. I think I had a tough day because Joe was having a down day, too.

We have done so well at encouraging each other. But tonight when he was discouraged, I don't think I was too encouraging. Comparing last night and tonight, I learned a lesson. Attitude really does play a major role in how our day unfolds. If we allow ourselves to be disheartened, and play the "woe is me" game, it only makes you even more tired and depressed.

I allowed Joe's negative attitude to rub off on me, and then I was downcast about everything all day long. We are human, and we will have these days, but it is important to look around, find someone else who is in the same shape and encourage them by uplifting them. By doing so, you will rise from the pits.

When you put this concept into practice, it really does work. Tonight I went next door to a little boy's room, who also had a head injury and talked with his mom. She was struggling with many of the same issues I had already worked through, and I felt she could use some company.

We had a really nice talk. I came back to my room feeling like my energy had been restored and my attitude renewed. God used me as an everyday angel to reach out to someone else and it felt good.

It's well past bedtime, and I need to turn in soon. The days seem to be dragging by this week. I think it's because I know we're going home on Friday. I am excited. It can't come soon enough. It really is time for all of us to be a family again.

God's Grace: Not an Easy Promise

Andrew is having a tough time lately. He just needs his mommy and his sister to come home. Michael is becoming very attached to me and has a tough time when I leave. Joe is another of my three boys who is very ready for me to come home for good. I have been so busy caring for Ashley that I've only been able to fit him in when time permits. Joe has been holding the fort down at work, taking care of the boys at night, and trying to schedule some visits at the hospital. He and I just haven't found much time together.

I'm glad we have a strong marriage because I can see how circumstances like these could be dangerous for a couple already on a rocky road. Being separated like this is very hard on a marriage and a family. I realize how important it is to have God as the third strand of the tie that binds a husband and wife. There needs to be grace and forgiveness, especially during trying times. We all handle situations differently, and it's important not to expect your spouse to deal with issues the same way you deal with them.

No one is perfect, and I'm glad we're not expected to be. It's important, though, to learn from your mistakes and ask God to forgive, teach, and guide you so you don't make the same mistakes over and over.

Thursday, June 29, 2000
9:30 p.m.

It's hard to believe I have made it fifty-two days in this hospital. Tonight is my last night here. We are homeward bound tomorrow! After Ashley's accident, the doctors said the first week would be very critical. I thought to myself, "Wow, I'm going to be here for a whole week?"

How naïve I was about my child's condition, or maybe I was still in shock. Little did I know seven and a half weeks later, I would be saying my final good-byes to the hospital staff. It's not like we'll be gone forever, we'll be back three times a week (or more) for outpatient therapy. I'm really anxious to see what progress Ashley makes at home. I know our family has lots of love and energy. Just being in her home environment should make a huge difference.

GOING HOME!

Saturday, July 1, 2000
8:30 p.m.

We are home! I can't begin to express how wonderful it feels to be home with my family again. We came home yesterday and as wonderful as it felt, I was too tired to write in my journal.

Joe and I both wept when we pulled into the development and saw a gazillion pink ribbons and pink balloons newly tied to most everyone's house in the neighborhood. Three large banners hung from our house saying, "Welcome Home, Ashley!"

The whole development, family, and friends have been very supportive since day one. We appreciate everything that has been done for us and for others in Ashley's honor. Her "good deeds" envelope is starting to bulge at the seams. Although we've received many good deed cards, I know there have been even more good things done in her name and not recorded. The love of people overwhelms me.

It's Saturday night. Ashley and Michael are in bed, and Joe and Andrew are off running an errand at the office. I'm sitting on the front porch swing watching lightning bugs flutter, listening to birds sing, and hearing the noise of a neighbor's volleyball game. I cannot look in any direction without seeing pink ribbons and balloons. My heart is overflowing with peace and joy. God has truly blessed my family.

Our family is reunited again for good.

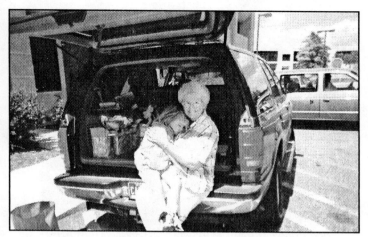

Grandma was there every step of the way.

Not only did God allow Ashley to come back home, but
He gave us a beautiful pink sky upon arrival.
Her favorite color was no surprise to Him.

Monday, July 3, 2000
11:30 p.m.

My days seem to be filled with soaring highs and abysmal lows.

Ashley continues to make progress every day. Yesterday she said "Mama" as clear as day when we asked her who she wanted to put her in bed. And tonight when I put her in bed and said prayers with her she said, "Amen" after I said Amen. It's so good to watch her progress. She'll be talking soon.

My lows set in when I see old pictures of her, or when I touch things she made by herself, or glimpse toys she used to play with. Right now, we are using a beanbag chair to prop her up because she still doesn't have much muscle control. She was, and is, such a sweet little girl. I continue to hope and wait in the Lord. God will renew her strength, and I believe she will walk again some day without growing weary. God is in control of this whole situation and has been since the beginning. Nothing happens without first being filtered through Him.

Our prayer that first night was that He would allow Ashley to live. We wanted to keep her with us so badly that we would accept her any way God saw fit. He already had a plan in place for her on that day. No matter how much He chooses to heal Ashley, it will be the absolute right thing for our family. I'm sure He still has many lessons in store for us, and so we persevere each day and find joy in all we do.

Oh, by the way, we just found out today that I am pregnant with our fourth child. I guess that explains why I have been so tired and emotional lately. Joe and I are both very excited about this new addition to the family. I didn't think it would happen, but I guess it will.

Tuesday, July 4, 2000
10:00 p.m.

God is really awesome. Whenever we take time out for Him, He speaks to us and reveals His purpose, His plans, and His will. I have been praying that He continues to reveal what He wants Joe and me to do. I sat down tonight to read my devotion, which spoke of being a witness for what God has done. The devotion's prayer said, "Father, show me how to witness to my neighbors and friends. Give me the boldness to reach out to them with Your love."

God has really been working in the hearts of some of our neighbors and drawing them close. After reading that prayer, I know I am to speak to them on Saturday when they come to Ashley's welcome home party. After pondering how I could be a witness, I decided to say a few words before dinner.

What should I say? Well, God was again faithful, and I filled several pages of what I felt He wanted me to share. I know I'll have the strength to read them on Saturday because I truly feel it's what God wants me to say.

God's Grace: Not an Easy Promise

Sunday, July 9, 2000
10:05 p.m.

I am finding it harder and harder to write in my journal. Being home is extremely exhausting. I don't find as many opportunities to sit and reflect as I did in the hospital. I am making a commitment here and now to at least be in His Word daily, even if I cannot write in my journal daily.

God is constantly speaking to us and drawing us close. When we are not in His Word or focusing on Him, it is difficult to hear His voice. Our lives become so busy that at the end of the day we're too tired for God. If He is a priority in our lives, then we should spend quality time with Him daily. After all, we fit everything else into our daily schedule.

Today was Ashley's welcome home party with my family. She is simply amazing! Last Monday she was imitating sounds, by Thursday she was repeating words, and by Friday she was able to answer simple questions. She has accomplished the therapist's six-month speech goals in just four days. It took more than eight weeks for her speech to come back, but when it did, it really did! Praise God!

This morning when I said, "I love you," she said those precious words I have been longing to hear, "I love you, too." I can't wait to go to her speech therapy tomorrow. Her therapist will be amazed.

We decided to tell our family about the pregnancy, mostly because we are so happy. However, the news didn't go over well. I think everyone is concerned about my health, not to mention Ashley's needs. They are concerned with the toll it will take on everyone. I was a bit hurt by their responses but understood their concerns.

To me, this pregnancy says that life will go on no matter what happened to our family. I can say without question, our future plans are intact. God has the whole picture completed, and I trust He would not have allowed this pregnancy if it weren't in our best interest. Again we trust and take one day at a time.

Wednesday, July 12, 2000
10:49 p.m.

Ashley continues to make wonderful progress. She is now wearing her little panties again. No more diapers (for her anyway)! She had a great session in therapy today. Her therapists were all quite impressed with her. She is getting stronger every day. We get through each day and are able to find lots of joy in it. God continues to be faithful and my source of strength. I truly could not be doing what I'm doing without Him. He gets all the glory.

Thursday, July 13, 2000
9:57 p.m.

Today felt like a roller coaster—full of ups and downs. Pictures of Ashley before the accident are so hard to see. When I allow myself to get discouraged, I seem to dwell on the old Ashley and want her back. That, I believe, is a normal human response to this kind of event, but one that will definitely get me into trouble. There are no paths in life that will take me back; I just need to move forward with the hand that we've been dealt. I'm very happy to still have her. God is doing an amazing thing through our little girl, and she is getting better every day. I need to remind myself to live by faith and not by sight.

Today, Ashley and I visited her old roommate, Ruth. It was a great visit for all of us. Ruth reminded me to talk with the Holy Spirit daily. She also said she thought God was blessing our family with a recovery, and planning to use us in a mighty way for His kingdom.

Monday, July 17, 2000
9:30 p.m.

It has now been ten weeks since the accident. God has truly performed miracles in and through Ashley. She continues to amaze us. The process is slow but the healing is steady. I continue to pray for Ashley's eyesight to return. I have seen some encouraging movements in the past couple of days. I don't want to get my hopes up, so I try to put her eyesight in God's hands and know that's the best thing to do.

This long healing process continues to teach lessons. Patience is a tough lesson to learn at times. God is using every part of this experience for His purposes. I pray *that God continues to use our family for His will. I'm not sure exactly what lies ahead for us, but I'm waiting (praying, listening, learning, and reading His Word) for the next step. As I wait on the Lord, I continue to share what He has done, and what I have learned as a result of Ashley's accident. God will complete the good work He began in Ashley. I pray the spark that was lit in the hearts of many will continue to grow as family, friends, neighbors, and strangers continue to follow Ashley's story and progress.*

Wednesday, July 19, 2000

Today was an emotional day. I'm sure my fatigue played a major role. It's hard at times to watch Ashley struggle with tasks that she never even thought about prior to her accident: things like picking up a toy, or trying to sit up at the table, or alone on the floor. I would take all her pain and disabilities if I could. I would give her my eyesight and make everything better for her. I would if I could, but I know I can't. I am glad I'm able to be with her all the time. She loves her mommy so. She also loves her daddy very much. She has been asking for him when she gets sad and talks about him throughout the day.

She and her daddy carried on quite a conversation tonight. Her speech is coming along nicely. Praise God. We continue to pray daily for her eyesight. I remember the devotion I read in the hospital that said: patience is waiting without worrying. It is so hard to do sometimes. Leaving Ashley's vision in God's hands is the only, and the very best, thing we can do for her. What would we do without an Almighty Father who loves us and cares for us more than we can ever imagine?

Tuesday, July 25, 2000
9:45 p.m.

Our family is on vacation in Ocean City, Maryland. I can't explain how good it feels to be together again and having fun away from daily routines and appointments.

Ashley loves the beach. She likes playing in the sand and walking in the water with her daddy's help. Getting her to the beach and back is a job. I can't wait until she is able to walk, or better yet, run to the beach by herself.

It has been rainy the last couple of days. Our family spent a lot of time together doing inside things. Life is definitely different for us, but we seem to be adjusting to the way things are. I feel very blessed in knowing that each day Ashley is getting better. As a mom, I would like the process to move faster, but I cherish each day and the accomplishments she makes. Last week she rediscovered her bunny and remembered how much she loves it. She needs her bunny and blanket again! Thank You, Lord!

Another "Ashley" trait that has returned unfortunately, or fortunately, depending on how you look at it, is her temper tantrums. We went out to dinner tonight with Joe's sister and brother-in-law. I found myself dealing with a very stubborn and mad little girl. I'm not sure what set her off, but I finally (after forty-five minutes) turned to God and cried out for Him to intervene.

I was at my wits' end and didn't know which way to go. (I wonder why it takes getting to that point before we turn to God and are broken before Him?)

After I'd prayed to the Lord, Ashley got over her tantrum rather quickly. Not only did she stop crying but she was in the best mood ever—happier than I've seen her in a long time. Some people might argue that my prayers had nothing to do with her mood change but I know differently. God can and does answer prayers instantly. He continues to walk side by side with us daily and desires for us to cry out to Him and bring all things to Him in prayer.

Wednesday, July 26, 2000
10:30 p.m.

Tonight was probably the best night for our family since that awful May 8 evening when the accident happened. We had a picnic on the beach. It was so good to be together as a family and truly have fun. Ashley talked more today than any time after the accident.

Joe carried Ashley from the beach, and she told him how she would run to him again when she got better. She has such a will to stand by herself and walk again. I know she will do it.

As I write in my journal tonight, Isaiah 40:31 comes back to mind. "But those who hope in the LORD will renew their strength. They will soar on wings like eagles; they will run and not grow weary, they will walk and not be faint." I think this has become my favorite verse. I also claim 2 Corinthians 12:9,10 that says that His grace is sufficient for us. We should delight in hardships and persecutions for when we are weak, then we are strong.

My devotion tonight was titled, "Love's Fearlessness." God's love is truly perfect. 1 John 4:18 says there is no fear in love, but that perfect love removes all fear. We don't need to be afraid of the future. God's love is truly perfect for us. That love will give us the confidence that our heavenly Father only wants our best and allows situations in our life that we can handle and He can turn to good for those who love Him (Romans 8:28).

Monday, July 31, 2000
11:00 p.m.

Yet another milestone was reached today. Joe and I breathed a sigh of relief when the doctor looked at Ashley's neck X-ray and said, "You can take the collar off."

Early on, the doctors said there was a chance her neck would not heal correctly, and they would have to fuse the neck vertebrae, and she would never be able to turn her neck.

Ashley was thrilled to have the collar removed, and she said, "Bye-bye collar!" The whole way home she kept rubbing her neck and saying, "Daddy, look at me!" or "Mommy, look at me!"

Andrew couldn't contain his excitement. "She looks like Ashley again!"

Ashley's doctor was impressed with her progress. He even offered hope concerning her vision. Talking with him brought back so many memories of those first two weeks following the accident. He reminded us of her condition the night she came in.

"I thought Ashley wouldn't survive," he said as he examined her. "On a scale with two hundred fifty being normal, she is probably on step five, but when she first came in, she was a minus one."

God has been so faithful during the past twelve weeks. He has carried us when we felt we couldn't move another step.

Our recent vacation was wonderful for Ashley. She made some great strides with her speech during that time. I love the way she talks so spontaneously and normal. It is a bit slow, but she can definitely say anything she wants or needs to. I am very thankful for her speech. It's great to hear her talking with her daddy or with her brothers.

Months four-nine

Friday, August 4, 2000
11:50 p.m.

As I lie down to sleep tonight, I keep reflecting on the past twelve weeks. God has brought us through some pretty rough seas and has used these events to teach us. Following the accident, the greatest lesson learned was the power of prayer. God heard the pleas of His people and blessed us with Ashley's survival.

As the weeks and months passed, I think the next major lesson was, and remains, patience. As hard as it is, patience is waiting without worrying. When we were able to put our worries in God's hands (and leave them there), we experienced a fantastic peace. I am glad we don't have to do this on our own. God continues to walk with us hand in hand. I know I can completely give Him my daughter for healing.

I think of how far she has come, and I am truly amazed. God revealed to the doctors the night of the accident that she needed a shunt, He told me that classical music was needed to soothe her, and He put the right doctors, nurses, and therapists in her path. I give all the glory to God for each and every portion of her recovery. When I read about other brain-injured children, and the issues their families deal with, I feel even more thankful and fortunate.

Ashley's mental processing and figuring out new things seem to be coming along nicely. Her attention span is great. She will sit and play with an interesting toy or puzzle for a very long time. We do not have the behavioral problems (with the exception of a temper tantrum every now and then) to deal with that are common to children with head injuries. She is determined to stand and walk again on her own. We are so blessed to be getting Ashley back.

My heart and admiration go out to those parents who find themselves in a recovery that is not as positive as Ashley's, but continue to find the patience and energy they need to care for their child. God has a specific and personal plan for all our lives. We need to acknowledge Him in every way, and then receive His grace to carry on.

My heart is overflowing with love and gratitude. Raising our three beautiful, and soon to be four children, is the best job in the whole world.

Thursday, August 10, 2000
11:38 p.m.

It's very late at night, and I know I should be in bed, but I feel an overwhelming need to write in my journal. I am so grateful to God for all He has done for Ashley. He is truly a caring God that listens to the prayers of His people.

Ashley continues to make progress. She is so determined to walk. Her legs are stronger every day. She stood all by herself today for a few seconds—not holding on to anyone or anything. Tears flowed down my cheeks as I watched her. She has come so very far. She is truly God's miracle.

Joe shared his devotion with me today. I don't remember the whole story but it was about a man who stumbled onto Satan's storage area. The man found that the largest amount of seeds to be planted in people were seeds of discouragement. He spoke with one of Satan's workers who said the seed of discouragement works the best to bring people down. He then asked the worker if there was any place this seed would not grow. The worker replied, "Only in a grateful heart will this seed not prosper."

When I become discouraged about Ashley's slow progress, I need to remember just how grateful I am to God for how far Ashley has come. We have our little girl with us, and she is happy and beautiful and getting better each day. What more could we ask?

Saturday, August 26, 2000
10:00 p.m.

All of Ashley's processing skills continue to improve each day. Today was the first time she realized she had to go potty before she went. Up until now, I had to remember to put her on the potty because she couldn't tell when she had to use it. She was proud of herself. It has been three and a half months since her accident, and she continues to show signs of improvement.

Ashley was a little better today than she was yesterday, and yesterday she was a little better than she was the day before. We have been delighting a great deal in her progress and that leaves little room for discouragement. Satan is not winning in this house!

I want to make a banner for Ashley that says, "I'm a miracle child. Ask me how!" I want to tell everyone how God has worked through our little girl. He has answered our prayers with His healing hand, and to Him I give all glory and praise and honor.

Sunday, September 10, 2000
9:30 p.m.

I haven't journaled in more than two weeks. Time is flying. I took Ashley for her follow-up visit with her therapy doctor, Dr. Ramer, last week. Knowing the severity of Ashley's accident, her doctor was truly amazed at how far she has come.

"We never thought Ashley would be a candidate for the rehab program because she was so low on the scale," she said.

Dr. Ramer added that Ashley is still within the rapid-growth window. It has been four months since the accident, and she thinks she should continue to regain skills quickly until eight months out. Then she will continue to progress but at a slower rate until she reaches the year mark. Of course, this is what the doctors say. I learned early on that I don't hold fast to what doctors say; I try to see my child through God's eyes.

Our Sunday school lesson dealt with stress and storms, and reminded me how God is always walking with us. He never lets us down. Joe and I know this, oh so personally. Without God, we never could have persevered. When we were at our breaking point, God picked us up and carried us. God is good—always. His love is perfect. He wants the very best for us. It's our job to stay connected to Him. Without Him, we can do nothing.

Friday, October 10, 2000
11:00 p.m.

It has been a month since I've written in this journal. I went upstairs to kiss Ashley good night, and many emotions enveloped me. She was lying in her little pink bed, wearing her pink heart pajamas, and she was all curled up with her bunny and blanket—a sight I wasn't sure I'd ever see again.

God has brought us quite a distance since May 8. He has held fast to His promise of never leaving us. He has held our hand each and every step of the way, just as He promises.

I am thankful for the promise reminder He gave me that night in the hospital when I saw an exquisite rainbow arch across the sky. Ashley is making a terrific recovery. She continues to fight back day after day. She's the most determined little girl I have ever known. God knew the personality she needed, even as He knitted her together in my womb.

God gives each child his or her unique personality for a reason. As a parent it's important to realize the uniqueness of our children, and then encourage them and discipline them without breaking their spirits. We called her stubborn before the accident, and now we think of her as being determined. I thank God He made her exactly the way He did.

Monday, November 6, 2000
5:00 p.m. (British Time)

Ashley and I are on a USAIR jet at this very moment on our way home from England. It's been twelve days since we kissed Joe and the boys good-bye and set out to explore a therapy program in northern England. The program is called Brain-Net and has some very interesting philosophies in dealing with brain-injured children. It is a home therapy program in which I'm taught the exercises and philosophy behind them, and then I do the home therapy with Ashley. I'm anxious to get home and get the program up and running.

We have seen some wonderful progress with her vision. As we traveled down a busy street in London last night Ashley said she could see the headlights coming toward us.

I look at her all curled up on the plane seat, sound asleep, and I feel blessed that God has allowed her to reach this point. We heard some pretty tough stories last week while attending the Brain-Net program. I am so grateful that Ashley is able to get around on her own, and that she is able to communicate with us. I love to hear her laugh, cry, and yes, even throw her little temper tantrums.

While we were in England, we received news that my nephew, Keith, was killed in an automobile accident. Life is so precious; we never know when our time on this earth will end. Life doesn't come with guarantees for any of us. I'm not sure why Ashley survived her accident and is making a good recovery, and Keith did not. Again I say, I don't think God causes accidents to happen, but allows them in our lives, and then uses the circumstances for His will, purposes, and ways.

Romans 8:28 says, " . . . God works for the good of those who love Him, who have been called according to His purpose." We do not have the answers to all the questions about life and death, but need to trust that He will use the circumstances of our lives for good, even if we never see the reasons behind what He does.

One thing I have learned this past year is compassion for others. There is much pain and suffering that we won't ever understand. We need to lean on the people God sends our way. I thank God for the overwhelming support we have in family and friends.

I pray God will give me the right words to say to my sister when I get home. I know that when pain is the greatest, words should be minimal. A hug and good cry together with my sister will be good for both of us. I will miss Keith desperately. We were very close.

My comfort and my sister's comfort will come from knowing he loved God and had accepted Jesus as his Savior. We will see Keith again some day. Losing an only son has got to be one of the toughest things to accept.

When I think about God willingly giving up His perfect and only Son to come to this earth and die for my sins, I am overwhelmed by His love and grace.

I pray that the light of Jesus in my family will reach out and touch many others so they too can see the extent of God's goodness in their lives, regardless of their circumstances.

Monday, January 8, 2001
10:30 p.m.

The New Year has arrived—2001 has begun! Today marks eight months since Ashley's accident, and I am thrilled to say she continues to make astonishing progress. Her vision is returning slowly; she has some vision in her left eye, enough to get around without bumping into things. We patch her strong eye each day to force her weaker one to work. With her increased vision, she has begun to walk again on her own.

God gave us an early Christmas present as Ashley took her first steps again on December 10. Although it took seven months to learn how to walk again, she did it with God's grace and power. As her eyesight improves, her independent walking will increase. Her right hand is also making a mighty return. She is just beginning to pick things up with a pinching motion between her thumb and index finger. Her communication skills are slow, but she can understand everything said to her and can pretty much say anything that is on her mind. Ashley's present condition is truly a miracle from God.

Joe and I feel blessed to be her parents. We have learned a great deal about gratitude. My gratitude journal says that true gratitude turns denial into acceptance, chaos to order, and confusion to clarity. That is so true! We don't have the Ashley we thought we would have, and there are many things she still cannot do, but when we look at her through God's eyes and focus on the many things she can do, we cannot help but praise God. We give God all the glory and honor for where we are today.

February 23, 2001
9:30 p.m.

Today is Ashley's fifth birthday. It's so great to embrace her and give her a happy birthday hug and kiss. Nine months ago we weren't sure we'd ever have the chance to celebrate another birthday with her.

Life is normal again. We do things as a family and go places just like we did before the accident. Ashley brings special love and joy to our family. I can't imagine life without her. She is an extraordinary little girl, and I pray God continues to use her life and this storm we've walked through to touch many people and bring them to Him. He is the giver of life and source of true joy and peace even in the midst of chaos.

Part 3

Lessons Learned

Lesson 1:
The Power of Prayer

Six years have passed since Ashley's accident. We have learned so much. God has taught us and matured us in so many areas. We are no longer the same people we were prior to May 8, 2000, and for that we are grateful.

God did a mighty work *in* Ashley and *through* her. He has done a mighty work in many other lives as well. When God takes you through a storm, He intends for others to benefit. I will always treasure and cradle in my heart the many blessings that have come as a result of my daughter's accident. We have learned a lot about God's grace and the supernatural power He provides to overcome anything we face.

Of the many lessons He taught us over the past six years, I must say the most prevailing one has been the abundant power of prayer. Prayer is a mighty privilege that God gives. I truly believe it was the immediate and heartfelt prayers offered at the scene of the accident on that fateful day that saved

Ashley's life. Through prayers uplifted by family, friends, and pastors, God defied the doctor's prognosis of death that was poised on the tip of his tongue. Great and mighty things happened and there was no medical explanation for them—except through God's intervention.

Through prayer, He chose to reveal His sovereignty through us and make us coworkers with Him. God, who can handle this world on His own, instead chose to partner with us in His plan for this world. It is hard to contemplate that the God of this universe chose you and me to be His partner.

Often God does not, or cannot, work until we humble ourselves before him and pray. God tells us in Jeremiah 33:3, "Call to me and I will answer you and tell you great and unsearchable things you do not know." Imagine that. God not only gives us an invitation to pray but also promises to answer. We need to acknowledge our earnest, heartfelt prayers have powerful results.

Psalm 3:5 speaks of David as a shepherd and the peace he received at night through prayer. The same peace that God gave to David thousands of years ago on a hillside, He gave to our family following Ashley's accident. It was a supernatural peace that transcended our entire being and gave us strength to persevere.

We found it easier to walk through our days and sleep at night when we had the full assurance that God was in control. Friends and family enveloped my family in prayer; their prayers were not only focused on Ashley, but also on each member of the family. It is hard to believe, but we actually felt their prayers and had an inward peace, which we couldn't explain.

The peace God provided reminded me of Jesus on the boat during the storm. The storm was lashing out, creating havoc with the waves; the men on the boat were fearful, yet Jesus curled up in the front of the boat and slept soundly. As the Son of God, Jesus' life was full of prayer, and He operated in His father's power. Like Jesus, when we pray, it's not necessary to be consumed with worry and fear.

The power emanating from the myriad daily prayers carried our family on angels' wings, allowing us not only to persevere through the storm, but to retain our peace, hope, and joy in the midst of it.

The day following Ashley's accident, a group of quilters at our church made a prayer quilt for her. Six to ten ladies gathered after the accident to sew the colorful quilt, which was made of small four-inch squares sewn together.

In the center of each square, some pink thread was pulled through, but not tied. When the quilt was completed, they took it into their Bible study room and prayed over it. Each woman took turns coming to the blanket, saying a prayer for Ashley, and then tying a square knot.

Since they finished the blanket on a Tuesday, the same day of our mom's group, Sonya Miller took the blanket to each group member to say prayers for Ashley and our family. They also tied a square knot. The blanket became a tangible reminder to me of the prayers that faithfully were being offered for our family. At the hospital, my mom also held the blanket in one hand as she prayed for Ashley.

An inspiration blanket, a beautiful checkerboard quilt with alternating pink heart and plain white squares, was also completed. At Ashley's welcome home party, I asked people to write how Ashley had inspired them on a pink paper heart, which was later transferred to the white squares.

I found great comfort knowing Ashley was well blanketed with prayers. It amazes me to think that God hears each and every prayer offered by his children. We serve an awesome God who promises to hear us when we call.

Ashley's accident brought many people to their knees. I remember the first night when our neighbor, Bob, came to the hospital. He gave Joe and me a hug. "I really admire your faith," he said. Bob looked beyond us, fixating on the wall. We could tell he was thinking about something that touched him deeply.

"It's been a really long time since I last prayed," he said, choking back tears, "but when I saw Ashley's little body lying there on the road . . ."

Bob had placed his hand on her chest, closed his eyes, and prayed with all his heart. Tears bristled at the corners of his eyes as he cried out to Almighty God to save our little girl.

The Psalms are filled with David, and others, who cried out to God in despair. Psalm 50:15 says, ". . .call upon me in the day of trouble; I will deliver you, and you will honor me." God hears the emergency prayers of His people. He desires for us to cry out to Him for protection; for healing. He is waiting with open arms to deliver us so we will honor Him.

I've often heard people say dejectedly, "Well, the only thing left to do is pray." Some people use prayer as a last resort and only try it when everything else fails. This is actually backwards. Prayer should come first. God's power is far greater than ours. It only makes sense to rely on it.

God's Grace: Not an Easy Promise

In fact, I was guilty of using prayer as a 911 call, but as I grew in my faith, God showed me great and mighty things through the power of daily prayer. Now, I am much better at turning to God before the emergency happens. Praying about situations before you embark on them will make a difference in how they turn out.

This is true in everything we do. God wants to be a part of our lives, and He wants us to pray without ceasing. Being the mom of five young children (we recently adopted a little boy from Guatemala), it is tough some mornings to get everyone up and off to school with everything they need. However, when I begin my day with prayer and worship, I find things naturally go better. We not only arise on time; we are up and out the door with time to spare. God, and only God, gets the glory; it's not something I accomplish by being a supermom.

Another favorite passage in the Bible is found in Philippians 4:6,7: "Do not be anxious about anything, but in everything, by prayer and petition, with thanksgiving, present your requests to God. And the peace of God, which transcends all understanding, will guard your hearts and your minds in Christ Jesus." My sister, Barb, when she was battling cancer used to repeat that verse over and over, sometimes slowly concentrating on one word at a time. Do not be anxious about anything. God calls us to pray about everything. He doesn't want us to worry about a single detail in our lives. He wants us to turn every situation, and circumstance, over to Him, and allow Him to handle it—it's called trust. I know it's easier said than done, but if you truly love the Lord and place your trust in Him, it is possible to find that peace which transcends all understanding.

God loves Ashley more than I do, and I knew He was incapable of making mistakes. I was aware He'd heard our desperate cries to save her. I felt a sense of relief, of serenity, knowing that Ashley was in His hands, rather than in my control. My often-repeated prayer was, and still is, *Lord, give me strength to get through this day.* Help me lay all my cares upon Your shoulders, trusting You with everything. Help me worry less and pray more.

Prayer not only is a privilege that God grants; it is the supreme benefit of life on this side of heaven. Through prayer, we can tap into the mightiest source of power available and talk face to face with God, the almighty Creator of the universe. We don't need to go through an operator to get to God. He takes our calls directly.

Prayer is vital to our spiritual life. Without prayer, our spiritual life would shrivel up and blow away. I believe one reason people don't pray as much as they should is they don't know how to pray, or they don't have a segment of time set aside for prayer. Because they feel inadequate, they don't pray at all. They are missing out on their ability as children of God to tap into His power.

God doesn't expect our prayers to be perfect—He just wants us to pray. Many days in the hospital I didn't know what to pray, or was so physically fatigued that I fell asleep in the middle of praying. I was comforted by the fact that my prayers did not need to be long and elaborate. They only needed to be sincere. I found good news in Romans 8:26 where God explains we have an intercessor who works on our behalf: "In the same way, the Spirit helps us in our weakness. We do not know what we ought to pray for, but the Spirit himself intercedes for us with groans that words cannot express." Think about this, The Holy Spirit takes our mumbled words and perfects them before they are presented to God.

Prayer works. We saw the awesome power of prayer many times during those first few months after Ashley's accident. There were little miracles that happened daily as a direct result of prayer. James 5:16b says that the prayer of a righteous man is powerful and effective. I was thankful for every prayer that people offered, but those from upright hearts were truly powerful. When we are walking right with the Lord, we can rest assured our prayers will prevail.

The Bible also says in John 15:7 that if we abide in Him and His words live in us, we can ask whatever we wish and it shall be done for us. Again, it is the Holy Spirit who speaks to us and guides our prayers. Through prayer our will is aligned with God's. God will never grant anything outside of His will, but if we are abiding in Him and are praying in the spirit, we can be assured that what we are asking of God is within His will.

Matthew 7:7,8 says, "Ask and it will be given to you; seek and you will find; knock and the door will be opened to you. For everyone who asks receives; he who seeks finds; and to him who knocks, the door will be opened." We can feel free to ask God for anything, but we must keep in mind our requests may be denied. God wants to give us what is best, not merely what we want.

I believe prayer is the tie that binds Christians together. Several of our friends felt so burdened to pray for Ashley and our family that they prayed whenever they awakened at night. They couldn't receive peace to go back to sleep until they were obedient, praying and interceding on our behalf. Have you ever felt an overwhelming urge to pray for someone? That compelling need or desire to pray is your assignment from God. Do not dismiss it lightly. Be in prayer for that person as much as possible. It is exciting to pray and see how God works through our prayers. God has given us the freedom of praying to Him anytime, anywhere, and about anything for anyone.

As powerful as prayer is, it is very simple. It remains a conversation with God. Prayer is talking with God and listening to God. It's based on the relationship between a loving Father and His son or daughter. Listening is the hardest part of prayer. We humans think we need to do or say something all the time when all God really wants is for us to be still and know He is God. The key to listening is becoming quiet before our Lord and King. God will speak to us when our hearts are right, and we're ready to hear Him. Sometimes we can't hear him because we are doing all the talking.

It would be impossible to build a relationship with your spouse if you never let him or her speak. Relationships blossom as a result of talking *and* listening. If we want to deepen our relationship with God, we need to talk less and listen more. God desires our fellowship. We were created to love Him with all our being. Deuteronomy 6:5 says that we need to love the Lord our God with all our heart, with all our soul, and with all our strength. It's through our prayer time that we draw near to God and He draws closer to us. It is during this time He is able to work in and through us to reveal who we are in Him.

About a year after Ashley's accident, I went on a lay witness weekend where God taught me a life-changing lesson in prayer. He taught me how to become quiet and

God's Grace: Not an Easy Promise

listen. Throughout the weekend, we had small- and large-group sharing. I volunteered to give my testimony during the Sunday morning testimony time.

On Saturday, one woman told the group that she'd asked God what He wanted her to share during her testimony. She said that God spoke to her about what He wanted her to say.

The exercise of asking God what He wanted me to say sounded good. So Saturday night after the worship service, I walked up to the altar and asked God what He wanted *me* to say. I bowed my head and got quiet before Him. God didn't speak in an audible voice, but instead spoke to my spirit. He prompted me about two things.

He wanted me to tell the people gathered there that He was good and that He was faithful. I went home that night and changed my testimony. I shared less about Ashley's accident and more about how faithful God was to our family throughout the year 2000, starting with my sister's death in January, Ashley's accident in May, and then my nephew's death in October.

The next morning, God prepared another lesson on listening. Paul Malinich, a good friend, was leading the worship service and asked us to close our eyes and just listen. We were not to say anything to God for sixty seconds, but just to listen to Him.

"Rose, I love you," echoed in my mind in that minute. I knew God was speaking to me simply because if I were saying it, I wouldn't have called myself by name. I felt God's love embrace me in a way I'd never felt before—intimately. I knew God spoke to me, and I knew He loved me.

I have had the opportunity to share my testimony many times since that weekend in January, and every time I speak,

I always go before God with an open heart and an open mind asking Him what he wants me to say. It is amazing how each time I speak He seems to give me a different message. The details of that day in May stay the same, but God always gives a different lesson for me to deliver.

He has provided messages about His love, faithfulness, faith, miracles, glory and honor, community, patience, gratitude, and loving life. There is great confidence and freedom in prayer. When I get up to speak, I have the confidence in knowing that I have prayed about my testimony, and I know the words I am to speak are from God.

Lesson 2:
Unshakable Faith

Ashley's accident was truly a faith-testing and faith-building experience. When we have a relationship with God, and we truly believe what the Bible says is truth, we trust in God no matter how dark the circumstances. His supernatural power in our lives gives us strength to live each day. It enables us to do things we never thought possible. Not only did Joe and I walk through the life-threatening accident of our little girl but we became stronger because of it.

Four days before Ashley's accident, I had attended a bowling banquet with several friends. We were a group of moms who enjoyed bowling together after the kids were down for the night. All of our children were about the same age, and we enjoyed talking about them. The Thursday before Ashley's accident, I had received her professional pictures back from a photographer. I told the group of moms how Joe and I marveled how beautiful and sweet she looked.

Somehow the conversation turned to accidents, and I said, "If any of my kids were ever in an accident, I don't know what I would do." I felt a shiver run down my spine, and I added, " . . . and if I was with them, I would have to be put in a strait jacket." That conversation took place only four days before Ashley's accident. I had even erased the memory until my friends came to the hospital saying they couldn't stop thinking about that conversation.

Some may say I jinxed myself, but I don't believe it for a minute. I know God knew what was ahead and through that insignificant conversation showed that, with Him, I *could* endure any hardship.

Faith is mentioned two hundred and fifty six times in the Bible. Jesus taught on faith often because it is the key ingredient for living the life God intended for us. We were created for a relationship with God. He loves us and will never leave us or forsake us. Hebrews 11:6 says that without faith, we cannot please God. Those who come to Him must believe that He exists, and they must believe that He rewards those who look to Him. God doesn't say that He will take away all our trials and tribulations if we believe in Him, but He does promise to walk with us and give us ample grace to endure them. He will always show up on our behalf.

When Jesus performed biblical miracles, He often told a person that their faith had healed them. Saving faith is trusting in the Lord Jesus Christ. I desire my faith to be like that of the Roman centurion who asked Jesus to heal his servant:

> *When Jesus had entered Capernaum, a centurion came to him, asking for help. "Lord," he said, "my servant lies at home paralyzed and in terrible suffering." Jesus*

God's Grace: Not an Easy Promise

said to him, "I will go and heal him." The centurion replied, "Lord, I do not deserve to have you come under my roof. But just say the word, and my servant will be healed." . . . When Jesus heard this, he was astonished and said to those following him, "I tell you the truth, I have not found anyone in Israel with such great faith."

—Matt. 8:5-8,10

It was the great faith of the centurion that healed the servant that day. In Ashley's case, it was the faith of those praying for her with the same confidence and assurance in God's ability to heal. I'm very grateful for the people in our lives who displayed a great saving faith. We trusted God with our daughter's life. We knew no one else could heal her but Him.

As I was studying about faith, I found a definition that said faith is the mindset that expects God to work. God doesn't need us to figure everything out. He calls us to trust even when we don't understand. Proverbs 3:5 says, "Trust in the Lord with all your heart and lean not on your own understanding . . ." We didn't understand why this accident happened but decided to stand on our faith and expect God to work it out for good. We didn't ask why us? Why Ashley? Or, why our family again so soon after burying my sister?

Through the support of my daily devotional for the summer of 2000 titled, "How to Survive the Storms of Life," we chose to turn the why questions into what questions: What does God want to do in this? What does God want to produce in me through this? What does God want to reveal about Himself to me and through me? How does God want me to use my trial to benefit others? When we searched for the answers to those questions, we found God and became strong witnesses for Him.

My family's faith during this time spoke volumes to people who watched from the sidelines. Three years after Ashley's accident, we had our last follow-up appointment with her neurologist. When he saw her that day, he was overwhelmed by how far she had come. He took us over to meet another doctor who had been on her case that fateful night.

Her neurologist tried to remind the doctor who Ashley was, but the other doctor said, "Oh, I remember Ashley. But what I remember most about her case was her family and their group of believers, expecting Ashley to get better."

Our faith made an indelible impression on that doctor without our even realizing it. We never gave up on Ashley because we trusted in God's ability to work.

God desires our faith be built from the bottom up—through prayer and our relationship with His Son, Jesus Christ. When your faith is built on Jesus, the Rock, it doesn't matter what kind of storm blows your way. The Bible says in Matthew 7:25, "The rain came down, the streams rose, and the winds blew and beat against that house; yet it did not fall, because it had its foundation on the rock."

If your life is built on sand, the storms will come and your house will crash. You won't be able to find peace in the chaos that you call your life, and each storm that appears will tear you down a little more instead of building you up. The best gift you can give yourself is to prepare for the day of affliction so your faith will not fail. Choose life and build it on Christ instead of wealth, success, or fame.

God's Grace: Not an Easy Promise

You will never regret the time you spend with God. It took me a long time to realize my Christian life was based on grace and my relationship with my heavenly Father. It was not my works that made me strong, but my true faith and love for God.

Our faith develops as we walk through valleys, and we trust God to be with us and give us what we cannot do on our own. When we are weak, then we are strong. Hebrews 11:1 says ". . . faith is being sure of what we hope for and certain of what we do not see." Two words that stand out to me are the words *sure* and *certain*. Being *sure* is believing in God's character—He is who He says He is. I know without a doubt that God is real. He is who He says He is.

I often say that anyone who doesn't believe in God has to see Ashley. She is a living and breathing miracle, and she's here today because God has a plan for her life. He isn't finished with her yet. The word *certain* means that you know without a doubt that God will fulfill His promises, even when you don't see the end result. A great example of this is Ashley's vision.

Ashley was completely blind for six months following her accident. The doctors said that because of the bleeding in the occipital lobes of her brain, she would never see again. I refused to worry about her eyesight and put it in God's hands. In November of that year, we began noticing that she could see light and seemed to be regaining a little bit of vision. Slowly, her vision continued to improve. Now, Ashley has ambulatory vision; she can see to get around and doesn't bump into things. She still cannot distinguish any detail. She cannot identify people or pictures, and she doesn't watch TV.

I continued to pray for her vision, and God spoke to me down deep in my soul several times. *Her vision will be restored.* He has spoken it, and I don't doubt it, but it has to be in His time. As humans we think we know the best timing, but sometimes God is asking us to wait.

During the spring following Ashley's accident, God began speaking to me about her vision and its restoration. I thought Easter would be the day. After all, it sounded like a good time to me. There is the miracle of Christ rising from the dead. Wouldn't it be great to have Ashley's vision miraculously restored the same day? I was anxious for Easter morning to arrive so I could see what God would do. You can imagine my excitement when we got up that morning and the first thing Ashley said was, "Mom, I don't need my glasses anymore; I can see better without them."

Could it be true? Had God actually restored her vision during the night? As the day wore on, it was clear that she still needed her glasses and still couldn't see any detail. Did I hear God wrong? Didn't He say He would restore her vision? As I reflected on these questions and her statement that Easter morning, I realized God was telling me to hold onto my faith. Even though we can't see how far her vision will come, He has spoken it to me, and it will come to pass.

In Mark, Chapter 8, Jesus restored sight to a blind man. He spit on the man's eyes then touched him. When the blind man opened his eyes he said people looked like trees walking around. Jesus then touched him a second time and his sight was fully restored. Jesus could have healed the blind man all at once, but he chose to do it in stages.

I believe this is how He is restoring Ashley's vision. God chose to heal her sight gradually so that His spiritual truth could be seen more clearly. Ashley's gradual healing is part of God's plan and must be in His time. Maybe God's time to fully restore Ashley's vision will be when she is in high school, and then her testimony will be hers, and not her mother's. I don't know when it will happen, but I continue to be sure of what I hope for and certain of what I do not see.

This world will always challenge our faith. We live in a fallen world and bad things happen. God allows hard times to humble us and prove what is hidden in our hearts. It is our choice how we respond to what happens. We can either trust God, and allow Him to grow our faith through situations, or we can become bitter and resentful.

My family's world was shaken on May 8, 2000, but I am thankful to say our faith was not. We clung to God and put our trust in Him. He has changed us from the inside out and made us new creatures in Him. It is amazing how God can take the worst day of your life and turn it into a brand-new beginning. Our family's new life in Him began as a result of the storm He allowed. When our priorities got in order, we started seeing what a true gift God gave us in each day. Our faith today is stronger than it has ever been. I give God the honor and glory for it. He is the author and perfector of life, and He loves me with a personal and perfect love that casts out all fear.

Lesson 3:
An Attitude of Gratitude

Gratitude is another lesson learned. When you are grateful for what you have, your heart is at peace, or as Paul says in Philippians 4:11, "I have learned to be content whatever the circumstances." Each day becomes a blessing from God. We can never retrieve a day once it's been lived. God wants us to enjoy the gift of life and be thankful for everything, right down to our cup of coffee in the morning. Many people muddle through each day in anticipation of the bigger things in life they think will make them happy: a nice vacation, a new car, a better job, or a bigger house. I have learned to enjoy life every day and to be thankful for what God places in my life.

A year before Ashley's accident, God started working on a grateful heart in me. As a result, I began keeping a gratitude journal in which I wrote five things I was grateful for. I was determined to fill all five lines, every day for a year. As I progressed toward my commitment, I slowly began seeing that God was changing me.

God's Grace: Not an Easy Promise

Most days were good and the lines easy to fill. The pages were filled with praising God, praying for my husband, and my children. Whenever I couldn't come up with five reasons I was grateful, God stretched me, and I searched even deeper. In time, I began to appreciate the little things in life like a warm cup of tea on a cold day or a phone call from a friend when I was discouraged.

My gratitude journal became a life-altering experience for me. When my sister Barb began to sink into depression from her illness, I stopped at the local bookstore and bought her a gratitude journal. I encouraged her to write five things she was grateful for each day. Some days she couldn't find anything good in her situation. That's when I picked up her pen, and together we went over her day, and listed reasons she was grateful: a smile from a nurse, the ability to spend extra time with one of her sisters during the never-ending blood transfusions, laughter of a child down the hall. Those things filled the empty lines in her gratitude book. She found she could be grateful for even the days when the storm raged around her.

After Barb passed away in January of 2000, my family found that God left behind a very special gift for us: one I will treasure forever—Barb's journal. Inside, we found two entries that she wrote in May and June of the previous year. God had inspired the words months before the family even knew her illness was terminal. Although at the time Barb didn't know she would be leaving this life to be ushered into the presence of her heavenly Father, God knew it—and left us a message.

I am thankful Barb was obedient to God by picking up her pen and recording some of the most beautiful words

I have ever read. When you read through her two journal entries, you will see the gratitude and love that spilled from her heart onto the page. Her words still speak volumes about living life abundantly and appreciating every day. The road she traveled was hard for someone so young—forty-two—but she journeyed through it with dignity and grace. Her trek revealed the majesty of God in and through her.

May 1999

The road seems to be getting longer rather than shorter. The healing process seems never- ending. I'm so thankful for all of my family, Bill's family, and friends in addition to people I don't even know who have been supportive through this illness. The amount of prayers offered daily is overwhelming—and I know God hears each one. I must remember to give my illness over to God totally for He will heal me. When I see the love in my mother's eyes, I know God gave the ultimate gift, His Son, so we may have eternal life. I could never repay the kindness and compassion shown to me by so many. I pray I can touch someone else's life the way so many people have touched mine. Let us never forget the gift of life and live each day to the fullest. We are human, but we are what we make ourselves. Each day, be thankful and kind.

June 1999

Give thanks for all the little things in life. Many times we overlook some of the simplest things that make us smile: the blooming of a new flower, a day full of sunshine, a smile from someone we love, or just being!

God has truly given us so much to strengthen us for times of trial and tribulation, and then He gave the most precious gift of all, His Son, so that we may guarantee our everlasting salvation. This world is not our home; we are just passing through. This sickness has given me so much to draw strength from, and I believe I will be able to conquer any obstacle that crosses my path. I have become a much stronger and determined person from this illness. God, family, and friends are what matters most in this world of turmoil. I give all thanks to my Lord, my God, my Savior for bringing me through this. All my love to each of my family and friends!

What a vast legacy Barb left us to follow. I read through her journal entries many times while I sat in the hospital awaiting word on Ashley. We learned time and again that having a grateful heart was the best medicine for our day. We were thankful our little girl was still alive. We prayed to God saying that we would take her any way He wished if only He would spare her life. He allowed her to live, and we needed to be thankful and make the most of our lives. We had to remind ourselves there was no road that could take us back to before the accident. It happened, and there was nothing we could do about it.

The poem Melissa sent me while I was in the hospital was a good reminder to look ahead, and not behind.

> *No matter how many detours you take,*
> *None of them leads back.*
> *And once you know and accept that,*
> *Life becomes much simpler because*

> *Then you know you must do the best you can*
> *With what you have and what you are*
> *And what you have become.*
>
> -Anonymous

I have carried those words in my Bible since Ashley's accident. I spent many hours reading the poem over and over. What it says is so true. How we chose to walk through Ashley's accident affected who we ultimately became.

The words of 1Thessalonians 5:16-18 became a goal for me. "Be joyful always; pray continually; give thanks in all circumstances, for this is God's will for you in Christ Jesus." I repeated that verse and personalized it for Ashley. It went like this: "Enjoy Ashley always; pray for her continually, and give thanks for her life, for this is God's will for our family in Christ Jesus."

It was tough to see Ashley with lack of muscle control following the accident, but once I took my focus off the machines and her state of mind, I was able to thank God for saving her life and for all He was doing to preserve it. The gratitude in our hearts allowed us to find peace, joy, and purpose in the spot where God placed us.

In our humanness, we learn valuable lessons from God, and then as time passes, we allow them to slip away. I'm thankful that the lessons learned along the way are so deeply embedded in who we are that they only require a gentle nudge from God to bring them back to the surface.

It took about a year and a half after Ashley's accident before she was invited to her first sleepover. Her best friend was having a birthday party. Kayla lived a few houses down the street and her birthday and Ashley's were only a day apart. They had been best friends almost since they were

God's Grace: Not an Easy Promise

born. Ashley was thrilled about the invitation. I dropped her off and watched her mingle with the other six-year-olds at the party. Then, Satan took the opportunity to pounce.

"Poor Ashley," he seemed to say. "She's so different from the other children. Look what you've lost. You don't have a normal little girl anymore. Look what everyone else's child is doing."

Satan's lies echoed in my mind, and I began tumbling into his trap, losing my joy in the process. But after I said goodbye and walked out the door I thought, *I will be joyful always. I will pray continually and give thanks in all my circumstances for this is God's will for me in Jesus.* Instead of throwing a huge pity party, I prayed for Ashley. I thanked God she could go to a sleepover without my needing to stay with her and care for her. I knew without a shadow of a doubt that my grateful heart had defeated the Enemy. I felt a rainbow within, and I'm sure peace and joy illuminated my face.

As Ashley grows older, Joe and I will be faced with good reasons to be discouraged. I know we will feel sorry for her, but we have made the choice to be grateful for how far she has come. That choice keeps us out of the pity party room. If we don't fill our hearts with gratitude daily, then emotions such as anger, bitterness, guilt, jealousy, and resentment will consume us. God does not want us to carry our pain and sadness. His grace is a gift given freely and abundantly to overcome all that threatens to steal our joy.

Last year, when Ashley was nine, our family went on a cruise. By all rights, she should have been in the nine-to-eleven year old activity group. However, that group was planning scavenger hunts, playing ping-pong, and having late night swimming parties—all things that were beyond Ashley's capabilities.

We made the decision to put her in the six-to-eight age group with her brother, Michael. That group would play inside games and do arts and crafts (which Ashley loves). But when she realized she was going with the younger kids, she cried.

"I just want to be like the other nine-year-olds," she said. As Ashley grows older, she wants to be with kids her own age.

The whole scene was difficult for Joe and me to watch. We *wanted* her to be like the other kids, but there was nothing we could do. Her accident had happened, and we couldn't change that fact. In situations like this, it's easy to let your mind go places it shouldn't. We learned that lesson several times. Feeling sorry for yourself, or your child, doesn't get you far.

Thankfully, we made a good decision and opted to be grateful. We are blessed that Ashley's alive and doing well. Only a few years ago, the doctor predicted she would lie in a bed staring at the ceiling for the rest of her life. However, God was in total control, and she is not in a bed, but on a cruise ship running, playing, swimming, and having fun. Once again a grateful heart was the best medicine for the situation. We signed Ashley up with the younger group where we knew she would have success, and she had a blast. She even made a good friend for the week.

Several years back, a friend gave some advice that has really stuck with me. Lisa has a grown daughter with disabilities, and she explained to me how she dealt with her daughter.

"I try to look at Heather's life through her eyes," Lisa said. "Heather is happy, comfortable with who she is, and with the life she lives." Lisa's child has grown into adulthood happy and content. Think about it: that's more than some young adults in today's world manage to attain.

I, too, try to look at Ashley's life through her eyes as well. She is happy. Her life is no surprise to God. He created her perfectly. When Ashley was five, she attended kindergarten at a Christian school. The very first verse they memorized in class was Psalm 139:14.

I wept with joy when I heard her recite the words: "I praise You because I am fearfully and wonderfully made; Your works are wonderful, I know that full well." Ashley is growing up happy and full of life just like her sister and brothers. God has used her and continues to use her story for His kingdom purposes. What more could we ask?

Lesson 4: Pursuing Patience

"But those who wait on the Lord shall renew their strength; they shall mount up with wings like eagles, they shall run and not be weary, they shall walk and not faint" (Isaiah 40:31 NKJV).

God gave me this Scripture not long after Ashley's accident. It gave me peace and hope that she would walk again. The more I studied the verse, however, the more I realized I was skipping over a very important part: "Those that *wait* upon the Lord will renew their strength."

Different Bible versions will exchange the word "wait" with the word "hope." Hoping in the Lord is expecting the Lord's strength to carry you through regardless of your circumstances. It means trusting God and being patient as we wait for His timing and the fulfillment of His promises.

Patience can be a difficult lesson. We live in a world that says faster is better: food is prepared and served in minutes, the Internet promises to travel the speed of light, credit card companies say why wait, have it now. The overall pace of life is in high gear. We want things, and we want them right now. There are many good things, however, that come if we wait. God may be using your situation to renew, refresh, and teach you something. It is sometimes part of His plan.

Patience is not the act of waiting, but our *attitude* while we do it. God continues to refine our character while we wait for His plan to unfold. When we accept an attitude of hope, truth, and joy, we are strengthened and encouraged. Waiting becomes less a burden and more an anticipation of what God plans to do.

Joe and I continue to wait patiently as God heals Ashley's vision. It may not happen tomorrow, but I know God has not forgotten about the promise He gave me. If our hope was in this world and what the doctors told us years ago, waiting would be unbearable. We would lose our hope, and would have no energy to continue. We would be irritable and impatient as we stumbled through each day.

After Ashley's accident, we wanted her healed quickly and completely. God, however, had another reason for her long-term healing. It appears that our waiting has been part of our training. God has taught us great lessons over the past six years. He has strengthened us again and again and developed us for our Christian walk.

The lessons we learned have been a result of our waiting patiently on the Lord. If Ashley had come home from the hospital after only a week and returned to normal, we would have missed some very valuable lessons God wanted us to learn.

Psalm 27:14 says, "Wait for the Lord; be strong and take heart and wait for the Lord."

King David was anointed king at the age of sixteen, but he didn't become king until he was thirty. God spent time honing his character and preparing him for the situations he would later face. While David waited, he spent time actively praying and pursuing God. God wants us to be like David while we wait. He doesn't want us to sit and do nothing, but to be strong, and take heart, using our time to further His kingdom.

Waiting doesn't have to be difficult. When you stay focused on the things of God, your attention shifts from yourself to others. "But seek first His kingdom and His righteousness, and all these things will be given to you as well" (Matt. 6:33). God knows the desires of your heart, and He knows the plans He has for your life. Be patient and seek out His kingdom. He'll show you when His time is right.

Matthew 24:45-47 talks about Christ's return. Christ will come again when we least expect Him. While we're waiting for the Lord's return, we are to use our time wisely. Our actions and activities should witness to others of our love for Christ. We should be actively praying, pursuing God, and striving to bring others to Him. If Christ came today how would He find you waiting?

Lesson 5: Compassion and Love

Learning true compassion is difficult unless you've been through a tough situation in your own life and can relate to how someone else feels. It is only then you understand how to help.

Before Ashley's accident, I felt smug knowing I'd been there for others when tragedies or crises befell them, but I realized there was a whole different and deeper meaning to the word "compassion" once I had walked a pit-filled road myself. The Bible says that faith without deeds is dead. If we say we have faith in God, and we believe in what He tells us in His Word, then we need to do what He commands. God tells us two things: to love Him with all our heart, soul, mind, and strength, and to love others as ourselves.

Many people showed their love for God and our family in the way they reached out to help. Their actions spoke loudly, "I love you, and I'm here for you." Love is not just a feeling of wanting to help but is the *action* taken as a result of that feeling. God wants us to put our faith into action and to reach out to others in love.

Our church and community revealed their love to our family in a big way. Every one of our needs whether it was physical, emotional, or spiritual was met by someone expressing Christ's love.

People from our church even planted pink flowers in our flowerbeds, and then cared for our lawn all summer long. A previous babysitter, who was in college, e-mailed and asked if I wanted her to come stay with the boys for the summer. Meals were prepared and delivered for months following Ashley's accident. The meals continued even after we returned home.

At home, I felt I should be able to manage things, but it was hard. It sure felt good when the doorbell rang at 5:30 and a friendly church member or friend appeared with a basket of goodies for dinner. I can never thank people enough for all they did.

Ashley's accident even pulled the community together. When I was having a rough time, I drove around the main streets of Elizabethtown and Mount Joy to see the pink ribbons tied in support of our family. The ribbons were also a reminder for the community to pray.

The pink ribbons originated in our development by a close neighbor who wanted to show he cared. Through his efforts, pink ribbons were distributed and tied around lampposts, telephone poles, and mailboxes throughout Cloverleaf Station. Our church and community picked up the idea and more than one thousand pink ribbons were handed out. The volunteers attached a small card showing Ashley's picture along with a request of support and prayerful thoughts for Ashley and our family.

When people heard about Ashley's accident, they wanted to help in any way possible. Praying for Ashley was the number one thing they did for her, but they still felt the need to *do* something else.

Physically, there was nothing else anyone could do, so Joe and I decided to ask people to perform a good deed for someone else in Ashley's honor. We asked them to write their good deeds on an index card and mail it to us. My nephew sent the first good deed card. He had helped his neighbor clean his pool in honor of Ashley. It made me feel warm inside to think that something good was coming from this tragedy.

Little did we know how much those cards would mean to us in the days, weeks, and months to come. Several churches set up collection boxes for the good deed cards; we had one at our house as well. Mail from the hospital overflowed with card after card recording good deeds being done on Ashley's behalf. We collected more than one hundred and fifty good deed cards. They were our source of encouragement on difficult days. On days that were especially tough, Joe and I sat together and read them. We were astounded by the things people did for others.

Tears of love and gratitude brimmed in our eyes when we read through the stack: dinners prepared for others, overdue phone calls made to loved ones, groceries purchased for an elderly woman, children sharing toys with those less fortunate, gift certificates given to those in need, trees planted, and relationships restored—all in honor of our little girl.

The list goes on; the good deeds are too numerous to mention. One of the most touching cards we received, which still makes me cry, is a testimony of the kind of love and compassion that surrounded us during this difficult time:

Rose, Joe, and family,

The giant sequoia is the world's largest living thing. They are majestic and massive, towering almost three hundred feet in the air. Despite their height, these giants of the forest have a root system that only extends ten feet below the surface. So what keeps these trees from toppling over when the winds blow? The sequoia only grows in groves with other sequoias. The root systems intertwine and interlock to create an underground web, and this foundation easily protects it from toppling in even the strongest gales.

People are a lot like these sequoias. We need our faith, family, and friends to support us when the winds of change try to shake us from our foundation.

In celebration of Ashley, Rye and Reed are planting a giant sequoia. It will grow and thrive along with two more trees planted for Andrew and Michael in a small grove of giant sequoias that are already growing at our place. May this living monument always be a reminder of the love and support that surrounds Ashley and your family now and always.

With Love from Ashley's little friends,

Rye and Reed *Morris*

God's Grace: Not an Easy Promise

The love and support shown as a result of Ashley's accident has left a lasting impression on me. This lesson will live on as I reach out to others the way people reached out to our family in the year 2000. I am much quicker to cook a meal or lend a hand because of what others did for us in our time of need.

I wish it hadn't taken this experience to learn this lesson so deeply, but I am very thankful I did. God pours out His compassion on us, and we too should help others who are hurting or in need. Often what might take a very little effort on our part might mean the world to someone who needs our love and support. God sent me everyday angels on a daily basis. People who cared went out of their way to show us how much they loved and understood. I want to be that everyday angel for someone else the way people were for me.

Lesson 6: Loving Life

I also learned a lesson about life. Each day is a gift from God, and He wants us to enjoy every part of it. Our family's priorities were shaken a bit in the year 2000, but all for the best. God, family, and friends are what matter most.

We have no guarantee how long we will be on this earth: some people will be here awhile, and others not so long. My nephew was only twenty-six when he was taken home. The thing I will always remember about Keith is the way he loved life. He always said to my sister, "Mom, you got to dance the dance and have fun in life." He loved everyone he met and lived life to the very fullest. Ripples of his love continue to touch people in great ways, even years after his death.

We are so grateful to God for all He has done and for how far He has brought Ashley. It has now been six years since her accident but still we know God isn't finished with her yet.

God's Grace: Not an Easy Promise

We celebrate life every year on May 8 when we have a miracle party for Ashley and spend the day doing things she enjoys. Our motto for the day is, "Celebrate the Miracle." We don't remember the events of that day in detail but celebrate the miracle and the life-changing lessons learned as a result of a short bicycle ride around the development.

Ashley's accident has taught us so much. We are not the same people we would have been today if we hadn't walked through this very difficult time. If someone offered to give Ashley back to us 100% the way she was before her accident, but we had to give back all the lessons learned, and the people God touched through Ashley's accident, we wouldn't do it.

Ashley is a special little girl. An aura of God's love seems to surround her, touching people in a special way. Joe and I feel very blessed to be her parents.

God has a plan and a purpose for her life (and for each of our lives), and He will carry it on until the day of completion when she will meet Him face to face. One day I know He will smile on her and say, "This is my beloved daughter in whom I am well pleased."

Not only did God save Ashley, but He saved me, too. Without His grace, I would not be the person I am today. He has an amazing love for me that is so great he sent His only son to die for me (and for you). Christ shed his blood for me on the cross and because of that sacrifice, I will not only live eternally in heaven but will live victoriously on this earth.

John 10:10 says, "The thief comes only to steal and kill and destroy; I have come that they may have life, and have it to the full." What Satan meant for evil in our lives God turned to good. He used Ashley's near-fatal experience to teach us about life. Through this storm we have learned to not take even one day for granted but to love life and live it to the fullest—every day.

I am happy to say I have not yet completed the race that God has placed before me. He will continue to grow me and teach me in His ways. As awesome as I think God to be right now, I know there is so much more I haven't even begun to see. God is so great and deserves our praise. Whatever I do in this life I pray that it will glorify and please God.

I was thirty-four years old when the light bulb finally came on. When I look back, I do not think I ever truly began living life until I began to see God for who He is. I learned two profound truths: one, that God desires a relationship with me; and the other, that God is always at work in my life. Surely I had heard these things before; after all, I was raised in a Christian home and went to church and Sunday school every week. But somehow these two ideas seemed as new to me as if I had heard them for the first time. God loves me, and He desires to have a personal relationship with me. He is constantly at work in my life loving me, protecting me, leading me, and maturing me. I was so excited when my head finally got in line with my heart. I saw God in a whole different way.

Since then, He has continued to open my eyes to deeper truths. The level of intimacy He desires for His children never ends. He wants us to plow deeper all the time. How deep we actually go is up to us. A daily prayer of mine is, "Lord, take me deeper. Remove the scales from my eyes and show me more and more of you." That is a prayer I know God will answer with a resounding "yes" because that is what He desires and wills for my life.

God's Grace: Not an Easy Promise

God reveals himself to us through our daily lives when we choose to seek Him, trust Him, and obey Him. It is He who builds our faith. Sometimes we don't like the circumstances and the storms He allows in our lives, but we need to trust that He is sovereign. God is everywhere, He knows everything, and He is all-powerful. He is in control. I know He will heal Ashley perfectly within His time frame. God did not bring her this far to forget about her eyesight or any other single detail of her life. Second Corinthians 5:7 says, "We live by faith, not by sight."

We didn't know how far Ashley would come after the accident, but from day one and through God's grace, we were able to trust in His promises even when the road was slippery. Through this trial God has taught us much about prayer, faith, gratitude, patience, love, compassion, and life.

My prayer for you is that you will take these lessons He taught us and apply them to your everyday life, and know that God's promises are true regardless of any storm you experience. His grace is sufficient—even when the road gets bumpy.

About the Author

Rose Block is the mother of five beautiful children, and she resides with her husband, Joe, in Davidsonville, Maryland. Her greatest desire and purpose in life is to honor God with all that she does and all that she is.

Rose feels the call of God on her life to go into the world and bear fruit (John 15:16).

Her testimony of what God has done in her life, and through her daughter's miracle, is an encouraging and uplifting message that testifies to the awesome God we serve.

Rose is available and willing to share her testimony at your church, school, or organization. Simply log onto her Web site at www.roseblock.com for more information.

Printed in the United States
65313LVS00001B/154-300